saying
YES!
to saying
NO

A Parent's Guide to Values-based Abstinence

Christy Baca

WESTBOW
PRESS
A DIVISION OF THOMAS NELSON

Scripture quotations marked NLT are taken from the Holy Bible, New Living Translation, copyright © 1996. Used by permission of Tyndale House Publishers, Inc., Wheaton, IL 60189 USA. All rights reserved.

Scripture quotations marked NIV are taken from The Holy Bible, New International Version®. Copyright © 1973, 1978, 1984 by International Bible Society. Used by permission of Zondervan. All rights reserved.

Scripture quotations marked NASB are taken from The New American Standard Bible, Copyright © 1960, 1962, 1963, 1968, 1971, 1972, 1973, 1975, 1977, 1995 by The Lockman Foundation. Used by permission.

Scripture quotations marked ESV are taken from the Holy Bible, English Standard Version. Copyright ©2000; 2001 by Crossway Bibles, a division of Good News Publishers. Used by permission. All rights reserved.

Author photo taken by Jenny Wilde:
Sprinkle of Grace Photography www.sprinkleofgracephotography.com

WestBow Press books may be ordered through booksellers or by contacting:

WestBow Press
A Division of Thomas Nelson
1663 Liberty Drive
Bloomington, IN 47403
www.westbowpress.com
1-(866) 928-1240

ISBN: 978-1-4497-5690-1 (sc)
ISBN: 978-1-4497-5689-5 (hc)
ISBN: 978-1-4497-5691-8 (e)

Library of Congress Control Number: 2012911704

Printed in the United States of America

WestBow Press rev. date: 10/31/2012

Acknowledgements

I am so thankful for the Lord and his continual grace. His faithfulness to show his love for me in his Word. His strength to help me press on even when there were days this was not what I felt like doing. When I sat down and did the work, he was faithful to do the work right alongside me.

To David—thank you for believing in me. For encouraging me to follow through with this. For never complaining on the days you came home and things weren't done. Thank you for asking me, "Did you write today?" Thank you for listening to me ramble on and on and on some days just to sort through all the words in my brain. I'm so blessed to have you by my side.

To McKenzie and Morgan—thank you for encouraging me. Knowing that you thought that what I am doing is important made this easier. Neither of you ever complained about the time I spent writing. I am so thankful for the joy you bring to me and for the stories you allowed to be used to teach others about the love of Christ through our lives. I love you both so much!

To the many who prayed me through this journey and were a constant encouragement all along the way.

To Amy Knight, for the "author's survival kit." You believed in me before I completely believed in myself.

To Dawn Dillard for your brilliant mind that put a name to this message by giving it the perfect title.

Susanne Lakin, my editor. Thank you a million times over for never giving up on me. I appreciate you so much.

The entire writing process for this book has been devoted in prayer. Thank you again to all of my prayer warriors and research angels.

"We must begin to believe that God, in the mystery of prayer, has entrusted us with a force that can move the Heavenly world."

—A. Murray, *Devote Yourselves to Prayer*

Foreword

"For he issued his laws to Jacob; he gave his instructions to Israel. He commanded our ancestors to teach them to their children, so the next generation might know them—even the children not yet born—and they in turn will teach their own children. So each generation should set its hope anew on God, not forgetting his glorious miracles and obeying his commands. Then they will not be like their ancestors—stubborn, rebellious, and unfaithful, refusing to give their hearts to God."

—Psalm 78:5-6 (NLT)

I am believing that the God of healing, the God who brings a savior to a sinful, wretched world to set them free, is a God who will write these words to deliver a generation of young people and parents from sexual sin that leaves devastating effects that last for generations to come.

Contents

Introduction

My mom was born to a sixteen-year-old and was given up for adoption. I was born to a sixteen-year-old and also given up for adoption. I have three siblings who were adopted—each one a result of an unwanted pregnancy or born to a parent not prepared to meet the challenges of raising a child. Premarital sex, unplanned pregnancies, the growing number of STDs, and the emotional baggage that comes with all of these things are the startling result of a lack of education.

My parents did not talk to me about sex. I knew that sex was supposed to be something you engaged in after you were married, but that's about it. I can recall reading a book as a young child—I think it was entitled *Where Did I Come From?* It was a book written for children that describes the reproductive process from intercourse to birth. In our home the book was left available for my siblings and me to read at will, but to my recollection, it was never read to us by one of my parents. It was complete with pictures. Looking back, I see the intent of the book was good; however, without the discussion of the information learned from the text, it can be startling and confusing for a young reader. This book has been written in an effort to share knowledge with parents about God's design for sex and to expose how the world has defined sex. I hope to share what we have learned in our journey as parents who started building the foundation for purity when our girls were five through prayer, books, and conversation starters.

Sex education is like driver's education—you have to have knowledge and preparation in order to do either with effectiveness without harming yourself or another person. You certainly wouldn't send a ten-year-old out to run errands for you in your car. You begin talking to them about the laws of the road as you are running errands. You use situations that come up as you are driving as teachable moments. They remember those moments when they begin to drive. Don't think for a second that I've forgotten how my grandfather taught me how to parallel park with two trash cans spaced apart on the country road just in front of our house. He knew better than to let me practice in town with "real" cars because I was going to mess up a few times and even hit one or both of the trash cans in the process of learning how to situate that Buick LeSabre just right between the trash cans. So why would we set our kids out to live life without any knowledge of the dangers of sex before marriage? On the flipside why wouldn't we want to be the ones to tell them how great sex can be in a healthy, committed marriage relationship?

Remember what I said in the beginning of this book—we are forever a parent; the relationship just changes. I'd say talking about sex with your soon-to-be married son or daughter is still parenting and a definite paradigm shift in the relationship. But you wouldn't wait until the night of the rehearsal dinner to say, "Hey, by the way, let me tell you a thing or two about sex." Why would we not want to be the ones to help them define physical/emotional boundaries in their relationships? Why wouldn't we want to be the ones they talk to about the unavoidable message the world is sending?

Please understand we are still in the midst of raising a fifteen—and twelve-year-old. There is no formula for raising children. I'm not writing these things because I think if you do just what I say your kids will be pure on their wedding day. The information I share in this book is meant to be a resource and guide for you to use as you see fit for your own individual family needs. It is truth to be shared with you and for you to share with your children as the Lord would guide you.

Chapter One

Be their Coach!

"Do not be deceived, God is not mocked; for whatever a man sows, this he will also reap. For the one who sows to his own flesh will from the flesh reap corruption, but the one who sows to the Spirit will from the Spirit reap eternal life."

—Galatians 6:7-8 NASB

Before we start this journey together remember this: you are either killing sin or it is killing you (or your son or daughter). If you have past sins, sexual or otherwise, take time now before you go any further in this journey and spend time with the Lord seeking forgiveness, freedom from those sins, and wisdom for this journey. Satan will begin attacking you every time you start to make another step toward putting to death this idea that sexual immorality is sin. He will begin to put thoughts in your head saying that your kids won't be able to obtain this lifestyle. Even Jesus told Peter, "Get behind me, Satan! You are a stumbling block to me; you do not have in mind the concerns of God, but merely human concerns" (Matthew 16:23 NIV) when Peter rebuked Jesus for saying he would die for our sins and rise again in three days. Trust me—Satan is on my heels every day. When he begins to attempt to whisper doubt in my ear or fill my heart with defeat as we are daily guiding our girls down the path less traveled, I say out loud, *"Get behind me, Satan!"* He doesn't have a place in the path of raising our girls.

Jack Graham, pastor of Prestonwood Baptist Church in Plano, Texas, and radio and television host through PowerPoint Ministries said this in one of his teachings on parenting: "We are imperfect parents with imperfect children. Being the best parent we can be requires consistency and training our children with daily teachable moments."

As parents, we can do our best to raise our children by influencing them and training them in truth. At some point they are eventually going to be left to make their own choices. It is our prayer that our girls will follow the direction the Lord is leading us in raising them, and our efforts will be blessed by their choice to honor the Lord in His purpose for relationships, dating, and sex. My husband and I pray they will understand they are a treasure and that they will protect their gift of sexual purity until someone is worthy to receive it.

Part of developing into an independent adult has to include a time of their testing the limits of their freedom. Our job is to be available and willing to redirect them when their choices aren't what is best for them and redirecting them with unconditional love and a healthy dose of grace. For me, allowing them to make their own choices is the hardest part of parenting. Especially when it means I have to watch them make the wrong choice. The following is a glimpse into how raising teenagers has brought me to a place of greater dependence on the Lord, because as they get older, my ability to control their environment, peers, influences, and choices is slowly becoming more narrow with each passing month. I think of the journey we are on as parents much like the job of a coach.

Confession

People ask me, "What has been your favorite stage of parenting?" Anyone who knows me will tell you I love my girls. *But* I don't like the tweenage/teenager stage of parenting so much.

This is an excerpt from part of what I shared with a MOPS (Moms of Preschoolers) group:

> As a mom, I have rarely had a hard time finding and fulfilling God's purpose for myself. I love my girls. I love being a mom. I love planning parties that fill our home with girls and laughter. Cookie decorating parties that would leave my house with red food coloring sprinkled on the ceiling of my breakfast nook! Tea parties that would start with sweet little girls sitting around my dining room table sharing "tea" and cookies only to end with half of those girls barefoot and headed to the pond behind our house. Having a child drop the Kool-Aid pitcher only to leave red Kool-Aid as if Jackson Pollock had created a masterpiece in my kitchen. Filling my days with a routine that brought me joy because each day was wrapped around reading together, playing with Play-Doh, learning to ride a bike, teaching Morgan to peel shrimp, or listening to them quote a Bible verse they learned from Awana.[1]

> But these days, I find myself chasing thoughts of self-doubt. I'm no longer the one they run to for a story. They know how to read, they know how to make Kool-Aid, and they even know how to plan their own birthday parties. So, what is my purpose as a mom these days? I'm the taxi driver to and from high school, voice

---

[1] Awana is the only organization with fully integrated evangelism and discipleship programs for ages two to eighteen that actively involve parents, church leaders, and mentors.)

lessons, basketball, student council, youth group, babysitting jobs, and wherever else they need to be. I'm the underappreciated cook, maid, and family physician. Trust me—being the cell-phone police does not warrant you "The Mom of the Year" award.

I get excited when either of my girls asks me to roll their hair because it means I know I will get at least thirty minutes with them in which there's a chance they might share a morsel of what's going on in their world. I'm the ear my fourteen-year-old will fill with weekly scoops from her teenage world. I'm the ride to the store for my twelve-year-old to get supplies for a school project. The objectives have changed, but my purpose is still very much the same: Fill their heart with truth, love, and understanding of who they were created to be. Teaching them to drive, to navigate relationships, how to handle disappointment, how to set boundaries that to them seem unnecessary but are meant to protect them. These are just a few of the objectives that are being taught these days. These objectives aren't quite as fun as teaching a four-year-old to read or ride a bike. I often find myself weary from the pace that comes with raising and redirecting our teen girls, it's a note from our twelve-year-old that reminds me it's worth it, and my efforts are not going unnoticed! Or I'll get a text in the middle of the day from my fourteen-year-old that says "I love you!!" These days I am in a different season that doesn't bring me the joy that I had when our girls were smaller, but I'm thankful that, no matter the season, I'm never void of the presence of the Lord and the Joy He gives.

I shared that little bit of reality from my own journey as an encouragement that this season of raising teenagers may seem like a dead-end street some days, but with the Lord we can find joy.

Write a prayer asking the Lord to give you wisdom on your journey of parenting no matter what stage you are in. This may be what sustains you when times get tough.

Chapter Two

Coach's Playbook-The Bible

"You will show me the path of life; In Your presence is fullness of joy; at your right hand are pleasures forevermore."

—Psalm 16:11

D o you have a strategic plan with which to guide your son or daughter in the right direction? The Lord is *your* life coach. The Lord has left a message that you will go back to time after time after time as you direct your son or daughter into making wise choices.

This passage is for your son or daughter. Show it to them. Help them memorize it so they will have it in their heart. It's a promise from the Lord that speaks confidence to the battle they are facing against the world when it comes to sexual temptation.

> Good friend, don't forget all I've taught you; take to heart my commands. They'll help you live a long, long time, a long life lived full and well. Don't lose your grip on Love and Loyalty. Tie them around your neck; carve their initials on your heart. Earn a reputation for living well in God's eyes and the eyes of the people.

Trust God from the bottom of your heart; don't try to figure out everything on your own. Listen for God's voice in everything you do, everywhere you go; he's the one who will keep you on track.

Don't assume that you know it all. Run to God! Run from evil!

Your body will glow with health; your very bones will vibrate with life. Honor God with everything you own; give him the first and the best. Your barns will burst; your wine vats will brim over.

But don't, dear friend, resent God's discipline; don't sulk under his loving correction. It's the child he loves that God corrects; a father's delight is behind all this. (Proverbs 3 MSG)

Tony Evans is one of the country's most respected leaders in evangelical circles. As a pastor, teacher, author, and speaker, he serves the body of Christ through his unique ability to communicate complex theological truths through simple yet profound illustrations. In one of Tony Evans's teachings to parents he says this: "We can't delegate the job we have been given as parents. It's not the school's job or the church's job to parent our children. It's our job."

In an effort to show you the Lord is faithful to lead us through the journey of parenting teens, I am sharing this story of Joshua and how the Lord directed him as he led the people of Israel across the Jordan River into the Promised Land. If you will lean on the Lord and seek his word for guidance, and follow the direction he gives you, he will be faithful to lead you through this parenting stage that some days may feel like a wilderness period.

At the end of the wilderness period, before Moses dies, he hands the leadership over to Joshua, who leads the people of Israel across the River Jordan and into the Promised Land. Sometime later, Joshua gathers all the people at a place called Shechem. He reminds them of their own past and the gods their ancestors served. He tells them of Abraham and Isaac, Jacob and Esau. He reminds them of how God set them free from the bonds of slavery, and took them out of Egypt, across the Red Sea, and to freedom in the wilderness. He reminds them of how God led them through the wilderness and finally into the Promised Land. After reminding them of all that the Lord had delivered them from, Joshua turns to the people and challenges them to decide what they are going to do:

> **"Now fear the Lord and serve him with all faithfulness. Throw away the gods your forefathers worshipped beyond the River and in Egypt, and serve the Lord. But if serving the Lord seems undesirable to you, then choose for yourselves this day whom you will serve, whether the gods your forefathers served beyond the river, or the gods of the Amorites, in whose land you are living. But as for me and my household, we will serve the Lord." (Joshua 24:14-15 NIV)**

In other words, if you are to say yes to the Lord, then you need to be able to say no to the gods of your ancestors. I have chosen to say yes to the Lord in his plan for taking the responsibility as a parent to share his truth about his plan for sex. I have chosen to say yes to develop healthy conversations with my daughters about God's plan for their future. I have chosen to say yes to the challenges that I will face as a parent when raising my daughters against the flow of the world. **I have chosen yes to believe the Lord has promised to equip me with wisdom and the tools to be the source of truth for my daughters in their growing years through puberty, adolescence, and into their young adult life. I have chosen yes to staying the course and**

being available to my daughters even when what I say to them doesn't seem to matter to them. I have chosen to say yes to the Lord in my responsibility as a parent and no to delegating my job as a parent to anyone else.

I have chosen to take the heat for my daughters if they say no to something outside of their yes. I am choosing to be the "Yes, I love you" for my daughters when the world says "I reject you for saying no to premarital sex. I am saying "Yes, you can have a party at our house" when it means my daughter is saying no to the party that allows for others to compromise their boundaries as young people. I'm choosing to be the "Yes, you can set your own curfew" when I see that my daughters have said no to the things that compromise their priorities. I'm choosing to be the no in my daughters' lives because I know there will be times when they will want to say yes but need to say no.

If you are to say yes to the Lord, then you need to be able to say no to the gods in the land where you now live. You have to choose; you have to decide; you have to say no to some gods so that you can say yes to the Lord God.

If you are still reading, then my hope and prayer is that you are saying yes to the one true God to be the parent he has called you to be in the journey of raising your son or daughter in a world that doesn't take no for an answer often enough. Know they will want to say yes even when saying no is best for them. Remember, the Lord is your life coach. His Word is a playbook for you to use to train your children how to navigate in a world that is issuing a battle for conviction.

Chapter Three

They are saying it but we are NOT hearing them

"Only be careful, and watch yourselves closely so that you do not forget the things your eyes have seen or let them slip from your heart as long as you live. Teach them to your children and to their children after them."

—Deuteronomy 4:9 NIV

Eighty-seven percent of teens say it would be easier for them to postpone sexual activity and avoid teen pregnancy if they were able to have more open, honest conversations with their parents. So, what are we waiting for? The numbers speak for themselves. Parents are living out of fear when they don't grab the bull by the horns and educate themselves on how to be the coach for their children regarding sex. Sex is going to become a part of everyone's life at some point, so why not be the one to teach your children truth about the most precious gift we will give to someone else for a lifetime? A healthy sex life has been proven to be a part of strong marriages. If we are not talking to our children about the harmful effects of sex outside of marriage, and they are engaging in sexual behavior before marriage, then they are putting themselves at risk to be a part of the increasing divorce rates in America.

According to US Attorney Legal Services:

- In terms of both divorce and marital happiness, marriages that were preceded by cohabitation are less successful than those that were not.
- 55% of different-sex cohabitants get married within five years of moving in together; 40% break up within that same time period.
- About 10% remain in an unmarried relationship five years or longer.
- The probability of a first marriage ending in separation or divorce within five years: 20%.
- The probability of a premarital cohabitation breaking up within five years: 49%.
- After ten years, the probability of a first marriage ending is 33%, compared with 62% for cohabitations.

When I speak to students in schools about abstinence, I ask them this question: "Who do you think is having the best sex—your peers or your parents?" Of course there's always a sudden burst of snickers and laughter and shifting in their seats. Then I very boldly say with a huge smile on my face (because they usually don't answer this question), "Your parents are!" I love it! I love seeing their eyes get big with complete and utter disgust. It's true. Healthy married couples are having the best sex because that's the way God intended for it to be. Reality proves different from what you are being taught by media and "safe sex" education.

"Contrary to pop-culture wisdom, those who do choose to save sex for marriage are not doomed to a second-class sex life. Rather, they typically report higher levels of sexual satisfaction and marital contentment. Moreover, early sexual experience has been linked to marital dissatisfaction, low self-esteem, and greater incidence of divorce."[2]

Healthy marriages produce healthy families. A healthy family has healthy kids. I want healthy kids, don't you?

---

[2] Jeff Hooten: "The New Virgins." www.troubledwith.com/Web/ groups/public//@fotf_troubledwith/documents/articles/ March 16, 2004.

Chapter Four

Knowledge is Power

The world has a way of mudding the waters when it comes to what abstinence is. Abstinence is the only 100 percent effective way to avoid STDs, emotional scars, and teen pregnancy. Increased abstinence is responsible for the majority of the nationwide decline in teen pregnancies. Just the definition of abstinence should be motivation for any parent to want to teach their child all about it. Right? Well, it is for some. Then, for others who are buying into the idea that their son or daughter is going to have sex anyway, they are going to go ahead and teach them how to use a condom or take their fifteen-year-old daughter to the doctor to get a prescription for birth control pills. Furthermore, a number of peer-reviewed published studies show that abstinence education can decrease sexual initiation, increase abstinent behavior among sexually active teens, and/or decrease the number of partners among sexually active teens.

Truth Wins

The investment we make as parents can have a positive dividend if we are depositing truth. It's getting past the awkward feeling that comes with sharing some of those truths that can be hardest. I was visiting with two of my friends one afternoon while our kids played. One of the moms said, "I read a book about sex to my girls recently. Just thinking about saying the words *vagina* and *penis* made me want to choke."

This is a common comment from parents. She went on to explain to me that she knew she needed to use the anatomical terminology when beginning the conversation about sex with her girls, but it just felt weird to say those words to her eight—and nine-year-old daughters. I felt very much the same way when I introduced our girls to the correct terms for the body parts of boys and girls. One of our girls laughed when I said *vagina* and told me it sounded like I was speaking Chinese. At the end of the second conversation I had with our oldest daughter, I asked her if she had any questions. Her response was, "Do I have to do that when I get married?" Although hearing about the physical act of sex sounded like something she wouldn't want to do when she gets married because she was just entering the fifth grade, I am pretty sure she will want to do "that" when she gets married—because God created us to want to do "that" when we get married.

We can't avoid the fact that sex has been damaged, but we can equip our children with the knowledge and God's purpose for sex by developing a relationship with them that creates a security to have ongoing conversations about sex. The Bible tells us in Hosea 4:6, "My people are destroyed from a lack of knowledge" (NIV). The Word is there for us to use as a compass in life. Take time to read, understand, embrace, and live the Word. Teach it to your sons and daughters. I love the way this passage (Psalm 78:1-7) is written in the English Standard Version:

> Give ear, O my people, to my teaching;
> incline your ears to the words of my mouth!
> I will open my mouth in a parable;
> I will utter dark sayings from of old,
> things that we have heard and known,
> that our fathers have told us.
> We will not hide them from their children,
> but tell to the coming generation
> the glorious deeds of the Lord, and his might,

and the wonders that he has done.
He established a testimony in Jacob
and appointed a law in Israel,
which he commanded our fathers
to teach to their children,
that the next generation might know them,
the children yet unborn,
and arise and tell them to their children,
so that they should set their hope in God
and not forget the works of God,
but keep his commandments.

The passage begins with a clear reminder to tell the coming generation of his Word. That coming generation is your son or daughter. Listen to the teaching of his words, continuing with the promise that he will give us the knowledge we need to share with our children and ending with a responsibility to not forget the works of the Lord, and most importantly to keep his commandments. Ephesians 5:3 (NIV) tells us: "But among you there must not be even a hint of sexual immorality, or of any kind of impurity, or of greed, because these are improper for God's holy people."

These Scriptures alone should be clear indicators that as parents we should be listening to God's Word, sharing his Word with our sons and daughters, and equipping them with knowledge and tools to keep them from falling into the trap of showing any sexual *hint* of immorality or any kind of impurity.

Chapter Five

The Why

When I talk to parents in the seminars that I do in schools, I ask them a question just to get their mind focused on what I'm going to spend an hour talking about: Why are you here? I can ask you the same question. Why are you reading this book? You want to learn about how to talk to your son or daughter about sex, right? In order to know how to talk to children about anything, you are going to be more effective if you are familiar with their world. When we taught our girls to read, we started reading stories to them that they were interested in, that were on their cognitive level. Doing this sparked their interest and helped maintain their attention span.

I'm going to move into that same method with this book by informing you, the parent, of trends seen in today's teens regarding sexual behavior, the influence media is having on sexual behavior, and health risks that come with premarital sexual behavior. And I'm going to equip you with knowledge of how to initiate the conversation of sexual maturity and the value of sexual purity with your son or daughter. You will also be seeing what God's purpose for sexual intimacy is based on Scriptures. I hope that the information in this section will better help you understand why you are reading this book and why you, the parent, are the one ultimately responsible to equip your son or daughter against the forces of the world.

Chapter Six

Statistics Speak Volumes

A ccording to a study done by the University of Texas School of Public Health, 12 percent of middle-school students surveyed report being sexually active at the age of twelve. Does that spark your interest? I was hoping it would. I don't know about you, but I have twelve—and fifteen-year-old girls who have not even been kissed! I can't even imagine them being sexually active. There are four girls pregnant, as I write this book, in our local middle school (seventh—and eighth-graders). No matter how young or old your children are, statistics are proof that there is another reality beyond the four walls of our homes. I hope that this book helps you understand the reality of the world and sparks your interest to be diligent to continue keeping up with the changes that come with the reality of the world.

This next statistic is my effort to *cheer you on*! Remember you are their coach. Be the influence they are looking for. According to the same source cited above, 91 percent of teens ages fifteen through seventeen that have not had sex said they were influenced by what their parents had taught them about sex.

STDs: Sexually Transmitted Diseases

It's not a pretty acronym, but sometimes facing reality will move us to change our reality. Dr. Meg Meeker wrote a book entitled *Your Kids at Risk.* In this book she addresses the very root of the rising numbers of STDs in America. She points the finger back at physicians, including herself, who thought they were doing parents, teens, themselves, and our country a favor beginning in the early seventies by making condoms, birth control pills, and other forms of birth control readily available to young people. Physicians thought they were decreasing the pregnancy rate and lowering the risk of pregnancies, and they were happy with that. But what they didn't realize is that with the liberal use of "protection," they were actually causing the STD epidemic we are facing today because so many young people were having sex at thinking they were safe from becoming pregnant, and that's all they were concerned with.

Canvassing My Neighborhood

In the year 2008 in Texas, these were the statistics for the four most common STDs:

- 3,353 cases of HIV reported
- 98,707 cases of chlamydia reported
- 31,569 cases of gonorrhea reported
- 6,321 cases of syphilis reported

Notice these are the cases that were *reported.* There are cases of people who have one or more of these common STDs and who don't know they have them; therefore, they have not been reported and their numbers aren't included in the statistics. If you want to know the statistics for these STDs in your state or your county, you can look them up on the Internet.

The sad truth is they were actually contracting and sharing STDs at rates faster than physicians ever imagined. Chlamydia is one of the five most common STDs. It is known as the silent sterilizer. Women have it, and they don't know it because it doesn't present noticeable symptoms, and then when they get married and try to get pregnant and have trouble conceiving or carrying a baby, it is discovered. By then it is usually too late. It can be treated with an antibiotic, but it's not guaranteed that the treatment of the symptoms will recover what damage was done by the disease.

The reality is that one in three students will graduate high school with an STD. When I go into schools and talk to students about abstinence, I go through and count the students by threes. I have one out of each group of three stand to represent someone with an STD. In a room of thirty students, ten are standing, and they get a clear picture of what that one in three really is. The ones who have been tagged as number three are mortified because they are representing someone with an STD.

Just how are STDs contracted? They can be contracted through the exchange of any body fluid. Acts such as vaginal, anal, and oral sex are all ways that STDs can be contracted. Some STDs can be contracted by skin-to-skin contact.

Oral Sex

More than half of all teens ages fifteen to nineteen have engaged in oral sex, according to a comprehensive study by the Centers for Disease Control's National Center for Health Statistics.

Moms and Dads, this should be reason enough for you to define the kissing zone for both your son and daughter. We have told our girls it is respectful for a boy to honor her kissing zone, which we have defined as the back of the hand or the cheek. Boys need to be told by their moms and dads to honor a girl's boundary for kissing.

Speaking of kissing, this just in: oral sex has been tagged as the new "Goodnight Kiss." Yes, you read that right. Gone are the days of first, second, third base, and a home run. Young people these days are going straight to the "alternate home run." Girls and guys as young as eleven years old think that they are not putting themselves at risk by choosing oral sex as an alternative to intercourse, but the physical and emotional effects are very much the same. In a documentary by Canadian filmmaker Sharlene Azam entitled, "Oral Sex Is the New Goodnight Kiss," girls as young as eleven years old talk about having sex, going to sex parties, and—in some extreme situations—crossing into prostitution by exchanging sexual favors for money, clothes, or even homework, and then still arriving home in time for dinner with the family. Oral sex is directly related to growing number of teens with STDs, but teens feel oral sex is safer than intercourse.

In the process of researching the effects of oral sex and how it has become a fast-growing trend among young people, I learned this from a report: STDs are specifically related to rising trends of oral sex. In its entirety, the report is two to three pages in length, but I pulled crucial information out to paint a clear picture of the direction in which teens are moving with their sexuality. Notice in the first paragraph the statistic that says, "For *one in four* abstinent teens, oral sex is the solution."[3] Remember what I pointed out when I introduced STDs? One in three students will graduate with an STD. There is a direct correlation here, I think. Oral sex is not abstinence, in my opinion. It is still engaging in a sexual activity with sexual organs; therefore, it is sex.

I have had multiple conversations with a young man who was proud to tell me he and his girlfriend are still virgins, but later I found out from his parents that he and his girlfriend had been exchanging sexual favors through oral sex because they thought that would still classify them as virgins.

Oral sex is an issue that has state health experts and student journalists fighting each other. The oral sex stigma hasn't vanished. A Tech High School teen said, "Oral sex—I don't see what it does for people." But for one in four abstinent teens, oral sex is the solution. A Pike High School teen says most teens "think if you have oral sex you are still a virgin." Oral sex exposes you to HIV, herpes, syphilis, gonorrhea, oral HPV, and Hepatitis A.

---

[3]   This report was written by Anne Marie Tiernon, in *Heath Reporter*. February 27, 2012.

Casterline says learning the lingo is crucial for parents preparing to talk to their teens. The bottom line for parents today is they need to understand that a practice they may view as more intimate than intercourse is now their kids' interpretation of "just say no."

Oral sex does not protect you from sexually transmitted diseases any better than actual intercourse does, although it does protect from pregnancy. If you look at the act of oral sex, it affects the same areas actual intercourse does—physically (there is a physical satisfaction from the act of oral sex for both parties) and emotionally (there is a bonding taking place because both participating parties are giving physically and emotionally).

The four most common types of STDs are HIV, chlamydia, gonorrhea, and syphilis. In the year 2008, the following statistics were reported in Texas: 3,353 cases of HIV, 98,707 cases of chlamydia, 31,569 cases of gonorrhea, and 6,321 cases of syphilis. Read that again, because I wrote that these are the cases that were *reported*. There's no way to know exactly how many cases there actually are because not everyone who has an STD knows they have one. Furthermore, not everyone who does have an STD gets tested on a regular basis.

If I could tell you one thing about STDs that so many people are uninformed about, it would be that there are two types of STDs. The first is bacterial, which can be treated and cured with drug treatment. *However,* the damage done by bacterial STDs cannot be undone.

The second type of STD is viral, and this type cannot be cured. The symptoms can be treated with medication, but once someone has a viral STD, they can never get rid of it. The sad thing about these is that most of the symptoms come and go in cycles. Someone can be carrying the virus for herpes and not know it until they have an outbreak. It gets passed on to someone else by exchanging body fluids or skin-to-skin contact. It is a very sad reality that dentists have reported having to call parents to the treatment room when doing routine oral cleaning on young people only to point out to the parent that their son or daughter has herpes in the mouth.

In her book, *Your Kids at Risk: How Teen Sex Threatens our Sons and Daughters*, Dr. Meg Meeker states that, "helping kids avoid sex is no longer a moral or religious issue; it is a medical one. If I didn't believe that we can be effective in helping our kids delay their sexual debut, I would stay silent. But we can help. You can help." The following are suggestions you can use in an effort to keep connected with your teen to help them as they are striving for sexual purity until marriage:

1. Understand that teens today face greater risks with the growing number of STDs. Being knowledgeable about the threats your teen is facing can help you help your teen fight against those risks.

2. Knowing your teen's friends and what they are doing with their friends is important when staying connected to your teen.

3. Listening is a key to opening the door of communication with your teen. Ask open ended questions and allow your teen to respond without interrupting. Waiting a day or two to respond with your opinion about a subject matter may be necessary.

4. Stay connected. You are the adult as the parent. No matter what they may say that hurts your feelings and may cause you to want to withdraw from them, stay connected. Even when you may feel like you are failing at every attempt to be connected, stay the course. Don't give in. Don't give up.

5. Stand firm in your convictions. Balanced protection from parents has shown to produce high self esteem in teens. When defining your expectations for them, follow up by reminding them that the boundaries you are setting for them are to protect them. Relate to them by sharing a time you realized the boundaries your parents placed on you served as protection.

6. Remind your teen that you are on the same team. The messages being sent through media and the culture are the opponent, not you. Remind your teen that you care more about their future and well being than the marketing companies or movie producers that are sending the message that premarital sex is good for them.

"For thousands of teens I've counseled, one of the major causes of depression is sex. I consider it an STD with effects as devastating as—if not more than—HPV, chlamydia, or any other" (*Your Kids at Risk*, by Dr. Meg Meeker).

Teen Pregnancy

Bill Albert, with the National Campaign to Prevent Teen Pregnancy states, "Overall closeness between parents and their children, shared activities, parental presence in the home, and parental caring, support, and concern are all associated with a reduced risk of early sex and teen pregnancy."

Let's take a look at teen pregnancy. This is the very reason I am writing this book. Teen pregnancy has played a role in my life going back to my biological mom, my adopted mom, and three of my siblings.

According to www.teenpregnancy.org, a site managed by the National Campaign to Prevent Teen Pregnancy, one in ten girls under the age of twenty—one million per year—become pregnant. (My adoptive mom, biological mom, and two of my siblings all are a part of this statistic.)

Eight in ten teenage pregnancies are unintended, and 81 percent are to unmarried teens. Again, I fall into this statistic as well, as do my mom and my brother. As I am writing this book there are at least four young ladies at our local middle school (seventh and eighth grade) that are pregnant. I spoke with a mom recently about some of the battles girls face at such a young age and how high school has been good but a definite learning curve for my husband and me. The conversations we have with our fifteen-year-old are constantly challenging us as parents to be aware of the environment our daughter is in based on what she sees daily at school. It's hard to avoid a conversation about sexual behavior when she texts you from school telling you it's awkward to see so many pregnant girls at her school. My friend shared with me that her daughter, who is an eighth-grader at our local school, was shocked when another student (female) just stopped her one day in the hall and said, "Hey, feel my stomach; it's getting tight. I'm pregnant, and my belly just keeps getting bigger and bigger." This is eighth grade.

Two things here: the girl who is pregnant doesn't know my friend's daughter but she just shared very personal information with her. And bless her heart, she's fourteen and pregnant. Where are the parents of this young lady? Where is the influence in her life that should be telling her she doesn't have to have sex with a boy to feel loved? Who is going to support her emotional needs and help her care for the baby when it is born?

Statistics are proof that our teens are facing a force we have to learn to stand against as parents. You have an advantage as a Christian parent who is seeking the Lord for knowledge, wisdom, and direction in raising your son or daughter. The Word is the very tool we have to fight against the force of the world. Deuteronomy 6:6-9 tells us, "These commandments that I give you today are to be upon your hearts. Impress them on your children. Talk about them when you sit at home and when you walk along the road, when you lie down and when you get up. Tie them as symbols on your hands and bind them on your foreheads. Write them on the doorframes of your houses and on your gates" (NIV).

I know that we don't all walk around with the ten commandments tattooed on our foreheads, but we can write them on a note card and leave that note card in a visible place that we are reminded of his commandments daily. We can be intentional to have a family Scripture reading time once a week. We can honor our sons and daughters with a purity ring as a symbol of their promise to remain pure until marriage. We can use daily moments to teach our children the commandments of the Lord.

Chapter Seven

Media Influences

"Do not conform any longer to the pattern of this world, but be transformed by the renewing of your mind. Then you will be able to test and approve what God's will is— his good, pleasing, and perfect will."

—Romans 12:2-3 NIV

M usic and media are playing a part in the decisions our teens are making regarding their sexuality. According to Crisis Connection, Inc., young teens (ages thirteen–fifteen) rank entertainment media as the top source of information about sexuality and sexual health. More research has found a strong correlation between the exposure to sexual content on television and the progression of teen sexual activity.[4]

Four out of ten teenagers say they have gotten ideas for how to talk to their boyfriends and girlfriends about sexual issues from the entertainment media. A recent report from the Center for Media & Public Affairs found music videos to contain more sex per minute than any competing media genre.

Just listen to the lyrics of most current pop music and you will hear some sort of sexual slant. Katy Perry's song "Teenage

---

[4]   www.parentfamilies.com

Dream" is a case in point—it has a catchy tune, but if you listen to the lyrics, you will be sure to keep it out of your iTunes library. I've gone ahead and included just some of them:

We drove to Cali and got drunk on the beach
Got a motel and built a floor out of sheets
I finally found you, my missing puzzle piece
I'm complete
Let's go all the way tonight
No regrets, just love

Look over the lyrics I have given you from the song. Set aside time to have a discussion with your teenager about what message the lyrics from this song is sending about relationships. How do the lyrics of this song contradict the values you want your son or daughter to have for their dating relationships? If the lyrics aren't convincing enough, watch the video on YouTube.

How are you as a parent reflecting the value you place on your children and their success of maintaining purity until marriage by the media you filter? Are you filtering the music they are listening to? Are you previewing the TV sitcoms they are watching? Are you previewing or reading reviews for movies they want to watch? Are you researching the literature they are reading? Are you protecting them from an accidental keystroke on the computer keyboard that could lead them down the path of Internet pornography?

Jack Graham, the pastor of Prestonwood Baptist Church and the voice of PowerPoint Ministries, the broadcast ministry of Prestonwood, says, "When you give God control of your children, you are giving him control, not giving up" (Courageous Parenting series). It is especially great to be reminded of this as we are raising children in a media-driven world. God's sovereignty is better than any protection we could ever give as a parent. Make no mistake, his sovereignty doesn't give us a pass to be a passive parent.

When teaching students in schools, I use some of the following things to talk to them about media and the messages they are sending about sex. You can modify these to use at your own kitchen table.

Ask your son or daughter: "Who tells you what is cool?" TV shows such *Gossip Girl*, *Jersey Shore*, and *The Secret Life of the American Teenager*, just to name a few, are defining what is cool for the majority of teens in America. Talk to your son or daughter about what these shows represent based on the content the producers use. You may even watch an episode or two of one or more of these shows to point out elements that are telling teens that sex is okay. Hang with me here. I know some of you probably think I've lost it. It's often difficult to get into the minds of teens and help them understand the reason we are restricting things from their life, especially their media world, if we don't get into that world and clearly define why we think a particular restriction needs to be put into place.

Ask another question like "Who or what in the media world says it is okay to have sex?" Some answers they may give are music, TV, magazines, friends, billboards, etc. Have a few ads from magazines that are advertising a product such as makeup, deodorant, or even food. Cover the name of the product the company is trying to sell and just leaving the picture available for your son or daughter to see. Ask them to look at the picture and tell you what they think the picture is advertising. You will be shocked when you begin looking for pictures as to what you will find. The motivation of these companies is to sell their product, but they are selling more than just their product. Are these companies going to be around when you have an STD, get pregnant, are depressed, or feel rejected because you fell into the trap of believing that sex is cool? Move into a discussion with your son or daughter about the ways companies are using advertisements to sell sex without even saying it.

To conclude this activity with your son or daughter, ask them this question: "Who tells you to wait to have sex?" Hopefully they will respond with something like you (mom/dad), doctors, youth pastor, brother or sister, teachers, peers, or God. What is the motivation behind the people telling you to wait for marriage until you have sex? Are they trying to sell you something? Or do they want to protect you?

The following are five ways teens misuse sex. Read over them. Take a few deep breaths, then pray about when you might want to talk about these with your son or daughter. They are examples of things I share with students when I go into schools. It is a way to open their mind to see what many teens see sex to be, then we contrast these with what sex *should* be used for.

1. *As a hook*: Some teens use sex to get a person to like them. Just because someone has sex with you doesn't mean that they like you; they like that you are willing to have sex with them.

2. *Commitment*: Eight out of ten first-time teen sexual relationships last six months or less, and one quarter are one-time occurrences.

3. *Ego trip*: Otherwise known as masculinity. Anyone can have sex; it takes a real person to wait!

4. *Convenience*: Booty call is a trend that's been around for some time, but it's just begun to get more attention, I think, because someone put a name to it. Booty call is when a boy and girl have been exclusive in the past but have broken up, yet still make themselves available for sexual encounters. Also known as "friend with benefits."

5. *Available to say they were your first*: These are girls and guys that make themselves available to others exclusively to be able to say that friend is not a virgin any longer. I know of a young lady that did this her sophomore year with a junior in high school and she got pregnant. It was his first time ever having sex, and he got her pregnant. She released her parental rights to him, so he quit football, stepped down from student council, and took a job. He goes to school and work and takes care

of their daughter in his spare time. His mother takes care of her when he is working or at school.

In contrast, this is what the Word says (NIV translation) about sex and what God's design for sex is:

- *For a husband and wife to seal the covenant of marriage and express the deepest level of love to one another* **(Genesis 2:24-25).** "For this reason a man will leave his father and mother and be united to his wife, and they will become one flesh." The man and his wife were both naked and they felt no shame.
- *To start or grow a family* **(Genesis 1:27-28).** "So God created man in his own image, in the image of God he created him; male and female he created them. God blessed them and said to them, 'Be fruitful and increase in number; fill the earth and subdue it.'"
- *For pleasure* **(Song of Songs 5:16).** "His mouth is sweetness itself; he is altogether lovely. This is my lover, this my friend." Proverbs 5:18-19 says, "May your fountain be blessed, and may you rejoice in the wife of your youth. A loving doe, a graceful deer-may her breasts satisfy you always, may you be captivated by her love."

Notice, the order I put those in? I began with sex being an act of sealing a covenant of marriage, followed by the blessing of starting a family, and ending with pleasure. I believe the Word is very clear that God had a vision for why he created sex. He was just as clear in stating what sex should not be used for. Proverbs chapter 5 is written to directly warn men and women against adultery. I would encourage you to read it and pray about how to share the wisdom in that chapter with your son or daughter.

Mary A. Kaisan, author of *Girls Gone Wise in a World Gone Wild,* says this about God's plan for sex: Sex is the testimony. Sex bears witness that God has made two one. That's why God restricts sex to marriage. If unmarried individuals are intimate, they tell a lie with their bodies. They testify a joining has taken place, when in fact it has not.

Another way you can initiate a conversation about the influence and affect media can have on our view of sex is to look for as many things as you can in one hour of watching TV that make the viewer believe that sex before marriage is okay or that media is a driving influence for premarital sex.

Just the other night my husband and I were talking after a show ended on TV and there was a pause in our conversation and I overheard a character on TV say she was a fourth-grade teacher, and she proceeded to write her name on a blackboard. As she spelled out her name, she said it out loud several times. Ms. Choksondick. Did you get that just by reading it? Pronounced "Miss. chokes on dick." This was a character playing the role of a fourth-grade teacher on a popular show called *South Park*. Ever heard of it? I had heard of it. I knew it wasn't appropriate for young audiences, but really? I was shocked!

Don't be afraid to redefine boundaries in music and media as you see the need. You are still the parent. Here's another little nugget of truth to help give you confidence: A 2010 study in the medical journal *Archives of Pediatrics and Adolescent Medicine* concludes that an "abstinence-only intervention reduced sexual initiation." A curriculum that taught the risks of sexual activity with multiple partners or outside of a marriage relationship and the benefits of waiting to have sex before marriage has been shown to reduce the onset of sexual behavior.

Are you willing to be the "Yes, you can possibly see that movie after your mother and I watch it first"? Are you willing to be the "Yes, I expect you to call if you are at someone's house and they are planning to watch a movie outside of our rating restrictions"? Are you willing to be the "No, we are not going to purchase that song from iTunes because I don't like the message it sends"?

Filtering Movies

A PG-13 rating doesn't necessarily mean that your thirteen-year-old should be watching the movie. I have included a sample of a review written by Pluggedin.com for the latest Nicholas Sparks movie, *The Lucky One*, rated PG-13. This is the sexual content section of the movie review: "Beth regularly wears a cleavage-baring T-shirt and short shorts. And when she splashes in the lake with her canine charges, that T-shirt gets soaked. We also see her wrapped just in a towel after a shower. Once Logan and Beth start becoming romantically involved, there are several scenes featuring the young lovers embracing, caressing, and kissing passionately. One sensual session starts in the shower (with both of them dressed) and moves to the bed (while both undress). We see them in underwear and also naked with critical parts covered by a sheet. We see sexual movements. A few times the camera takes notice of them as they fondle each other's (mostly) clothed backsides.

Beth reveals that she got pregnant while in high school. She immediately married Keith but ended up divorcing him because of his cheating ways." In the concluding remarks they wrote: "For all of its plusses, though, this pick has a big flaw that all too often comes part and parcel with romantic tales of this sort: Once the pretty leads realize just how perfect they are for each other, they can't help jumping into bed. Those steamy embraces and late-night caresses may aptly illustrate the sensual passion involved, but they set up an unnecessary easy-sexing worldview. And they certainly lend the wrong advice to any teen girls just hoping for a little hug-your-pillow romance."

The Lucky One came out as I was wrapping up the final touches on this book. The night the movie was released, my husband and I took our girls to see *The Three Stooges* in an effort to create a family outing and to distract our fifteen-year-old from the fact that she wasn't sitting in the theater next to ours with her friends watching a movie with elements that were exposing more of what the world wants teens to buy into: "an unnecessary easy-sexing worldview".

Make it a habit to preview and read Christian reviews of any and all visual media your son or daughter wants to view. Pluggedin.com is a site sponsored by Focus on the Family and they provide excellent reviews of movies, DVDs, and music. We started this practice early, so the standard was in place before we had to face the music. Our oldest attended a slumber party in the sixth grade, and we were pleased when she called to ask if she could watch a movie. She knew to question because we were very open to talking about what we thought was appropriate. It's not easy, I'll tell you firsthand. Raising two girls is especially challenging as they enter high school. We spend some of our "couple date nights" not watching movies we might want to see but previewing a movie that our teenager wants to see, simply to develop our own review of the movie. It's worth it, though.

An investment we made when our girls were young was in purchasing a Clear Play DVD player. Clear Play is a company that has come up with a brilliant concept, in my opinion. You purchase their DVD player and pay a fee to receive filters for movies that are on DVD. You can download the filters from your computer onto a jump drive that goes into the DVD player. Before you play the DVD you want to watch, you can put filtering options on the movie that cuts out things like offensive language, sexual content, violence, and others. We have found this to be a very valuable purchase simply because we all love to watch movies with great story lines. However, oftentimes those movies with a great story line may be flecked with tainted elements that the movie doesn't need to make it a good movie. Clear Play does not spend any money on outside advertising. They are dependent on the word of their consumers to sell their product. So, if you decide to purchase a Clear Play and love it—and I'm sure you will—spread the word!

Pornography

Forty-seven percent of Christians admit that pornography is a major problem in their homes, according to Internet Filter Review in their article "Pornography Statistics 2003."

> Today there is an increase in the access to pornography. Twelve percent of websites available are pornographic. The US is the top producer of pornographic web pages by far with 244,661,900 pages (or 89 percent). According to compiled numbers from respected news and research organizations, every second $3,075.64 is being spent on pornography. Every second 28,258 Internet users are viewing pornography. In that same second 372 Internet users are typing adult search terms into search engines. Every thirty-nine minutes a new pornographic video is being created in the US.[5]

Eleven is the average age at which most children are exposed to their first pornographic image(s). Gone are the days of sneaking Dad's *Playboy* magazine; kids being raised in the twenty-first century have instant access to porn on their smartphones and home computer. One wrong keystroke in a Google search can take a person to a site on the Internet with images that are nearly impossible to erase from the mind. Entering the world of pornography for some people is like opening a bag of Lays potato chips. It is an addiction that is extremely difficult to walk away from. Every time someone looks at a pornographic image, they grow more desensitized to pornography.

---

[5]   "Internet Pornography Statistics" (an online article) by Jerry Ropelato; 2012

How do you address pornography from a biblical perspective? Let's take a look at Matthew 6:22, "The eye is the lamp of the body. If your eyes are good, your whole body will be full of light." If we keep our eyes from looking at naked people, or people engaged in sexual or romantic acts beyond a casual hug or kiss, we are protecting our mind from thinking about inappropriate things and our hearts from developing inappropriate desires.

Prepare your son or daughter by telling them that you understand there may be times when they may be in a situation in which they are tempted to look at an inappropriate picture. They may feel pressure from their friends to look. Their peers may say something like, "Just take one look—it's not going to hurt anything." Remind them that God sees all we do and he is willing to help us out of a situation that is causing us to be tempted. They have to have the integrity to do the right thing. When they are tempted, God will show them a way out so that they will not give into it (1 Corinthians 10:13 NLT).

Mom and Dad, if your son or daughter should confess a time they have seen an inappropriate image, do not overreact and get angry with them. Take a deep breath and spend time talking to your son or daughter about the situation. Remind your son or daughter that you are there for them to talk to about this at any time. Most importantly, pray with your son or daughter leaving them with a feeling of peace and hope instead of condemnation.

Parents, protect your son or daughter from falling into an unnecessary trap, and protect their phone and all your home computers from that accidental keystroke with Safe Eyes or some other babysitting software.

Some of the best software filtering options are Net Nanny Parental Controls, McAfee Safe Eyes, McAfee family protection, PureSight PC, & CYBER sitter. You can also go to http://internet-filter-review.toptenreviews.com/ for the complete top-ten list and reviews for each product.

Chapter Eight

Sexting: It Isn't Just Child's Play

"Do not offer the parts of your body to sin, as instruments of wickedness, but rather offer yourselves to God, as those who have been brought from death to life, and offer the parts of your body to him as instruments of righteousness."

—Romans 6:13 NIV

Sexting is the sending of sexually explicit photographs or messages via mobile phone (Oxford Online Dictionary definition). Oh, but that's not all the Oxford Online Dictionary had to say about texting. Just below the definition was this phrase: "Like it or not, sexting is a part of growing up in 2010." We can't deny that it is happening. But we can choose to not be a part of it. Sexting is putting kids at risk for being exploited, harassed, and even charged felonies. Surveys show that 20-60 percent of teens are doing it: "sexting." According to Susan Lipkins, a psychologist who specializes in bullying and hazing, sexting is a trend that teens think is just another way to flirt. The reality is it's often used to gain recognition, improve social status, or hurt or harass someone. Sexting is a new way that teens are relating to themselves sexually. It is one more thing parents need to be informed about. Parents need to be able to respond to it by keeping ahead of the trends that come with technology and equipping their children to be responsible with their phones, in an effort to keep them from falling into the trap it can be. In the article "Is your child sexting? What Parents Need to Know," it says:

> "It's an abrupt change that's uncomfortable and scary to adults," she concedes, but says parents need to look at the trend as an expression of larger changes in the way teens and young adults relate sexually. "It's really an expression of the kinds of sexual behavior they're having," she says, noting that young people today may be more interested in casual sex than relationships, in contrast to past generations. "Sexting is just a reflection of what's actually going on."

Sexting can result in felony charges and in some cases cause for teens being charged with child pornography. "Although the legal system is slapping teens with outsized charges for sexting behavior, it's the real predators we should worry about," says Richard Guerry, executive director of the Institute for Responsible Online and Cell Phone Communication. In the article "Is Your Child Sexting? What Parents Need to Know" by Rose Garrett, Guerry warns that private videos and photos are increasingly becoming stolen fodder for sexually suggestive or explicit websites and blogs, even when the personal content is password protected or saved on a private hard drive. "The consequences of 'sextcasting,' the wider dissemination of images and videos across the Internet, are far more serious than those of simple camera-phone messaging," says Guerry. "Sexting is limited to cell phones and is really a method of 'sextcasting,' which is a much larger issue." Parents and lawmakers worried about sexting are already behind the times, says Guerry, who says that where previously parents worried about keeping kids from stumbling across online pornography sites, now they should be worrying about preventing children from becoming unwitting "content providers."

"It's easy to vilify sexting as an out-of-control trend to be stopped at all costs. But parents should consider sexting in the larger context of the changing sexual and technological attitudes of the next generation. "We need to really take a step back and look at it and understand it," says Lipkins, who thinks of sexting as a symptom, not a source, of teen sexual attitudes. Lipkins says that prosecuting kids for sexting behavior is a misguided approach to a new problem that's best solved the old-fashioned way: by communicating with your child about risks and teaching responsible behavior. "Parents have to talk about sexting behavior as a part of other behaviors, and really try to have kids learn how to navigate this world without us, because we're not going to be around forever," says Lipkins. Today's teens have to be taught how to make healthy decisions on their own.

A few examples of some texting acronyms that teens are using:

1. ASL=age sex location
2. ASLP=Age sex location picture
3. BF=boyfriend
4. GF=girlfriend
5. CD9=parents are around
6. TDTM=talk dirty to me
7. NIFOC=naked in front of computer
8. (L)MIL=lets meet in real life
9. HSWM=have sex with me
10. GNOC=get naked on cam[6]

---

[6] http://telephone-voice.factoidz.com/texting-30-teen-slangs-parents-should-know-of-text-messaging-abbreviations/

How do we as parents protect our teens from this? What message are we sending with the boundaries we are placing on our sons or daughters when it comes to texting and its limitations? How do we help our son or daughter become a part of a solution in an effort to create a decline in the activity of sexting? Here are few things you can do:

Communication: Asking them right out, "Are you sexting?" is probably not going to give you access to an ongoing conversation with your teen about sexting. However, staying up to date about their relationships by random text checks or frequent conversations with them about their relationships can give you an idea of your son or daughter's social life, and they will be more likely to open up to you when you have reason for concern if you are consistently in their world of relationships.

Become aware of the risks: The lack of neurological development of the teen brain is cause for them more likely to be impulsive and unaware of the dangers of sexting. Having a conversation with your son or daughter about the risks involved with sexting may be uncomfortable for parents, but moving past the uncomfortable reality of having the conversation can very well save them from school-wide embarrassment, legal consequences, and viral distribution of images or dialogue. Talking to them about the risks of sexting and teaching them to think twice before hitting the Send button for any message they create or one they may have received is a very good place to start.

Show empathy for the innocent: Sexting is not just happening when someone sends sexts, it also occurs when others are receiving a sext message, forwarding it to others, and contributing to an unknown situation of gossiping or bullying. Ask your son or daughter to think about how it would feel if someone else forwarded an image of them to someone else? Encourage your son or daughter to think before forwarding sexual images or dialogue from other people. Teaching empathy may be just what your child needs to help them choose to delete an inappropriate message rather than forwarding it.

Teach twenty-first-century responsibility: Your son or daughter may be a model citizen off-line, but anyone is prey to making mistakes online if they are not taught about the risks that come with certain behavior. It is imperative that parents teach their sons and daughters that anything shared online or sent through cell phones or e-mails can be saved and shared on the Internet. Anyone can see content that is shared online: friends, parents, teachers, strangers, enemies, future spouses, and future employers. Teaching twenty-first-century responsibility with the use of a cell phone is essential to protecting your child from falling prey to the trend of sending, receiving, or sharing inappropriate images or messages with their cell phone. Who is in the driver's seat of the media-driven world? You or the world?

When teaching your son or daughter twenty-first-century responsibility, you have to be up to date with the texting lingo as a parent. Several sites you can go to find out more about texting acronyms and other risky behavior that come with texting include the following:

1. Web-Speak101 for Parents: How to Decode Teen Text Online Slang
2. www.teenchatdecoder.com (teen speak translation made easy)
3. www.dtxtrapp.com
4. http://neenmachine.com/2010/09/29/decoding-your-teens-text-lingo/

Rose Garrett concludes her article by saying, "The best way for parents to keep kids safe is still to send a message of their own, which emphasizes responsibility, explains the risks, and keeps the lines of communication open."

Our oldest daughter, who is now fifteen, received her first phone the summer she went into the eighth grade. We gave her a phone that has Internet access and can send pictures and text and do some pretty cool things. But we only activated the texting and call features. She can use the camera to take fun, silly pictures of her and her friends. They can't be posted to the Internet or texted to anyone else from her phone. You have to decide what you think your son or daughter is responsible using. The smartphones today have so many great features that come with plans that you can control. Most plan providers have levels of parental control you can set up that is exclusive to each phone on your plan.

Recently, I sat next to a mom at a basketball game. She shared with me that her twelve-year-old son had received a text from a girl who was wearing a G-string. What that young girl doesn't know is that the one text she sent to that one boy could possibly be sent to other boys, and before you know it end up on the internet. Thankfully this mom deleted the image from her son's phone so it wouldn't have the possibility of being sent on to anyone else.

For teens, sexting has become a means to communicate their desire for casual sexual relationships. What so many teens don't realize is that the effects of sexting may surface after the relationship has ended. Suicide has been noted as just one result of a young lady sending her boyfriend a nude image of herself while dating in high school. After breaking up with her boyfriend, he sent the image to hundreds of others in their high school. Thankfully the mom I was sitting next to at that basketball game made certain that image was deleted. By deleting the image that had been sent to her son, she was keeping him from being drawn into possible pornography, and she was protecting that young lady from further humiliation at the hands of her son.

Sexting can range from incidents that some teen health experts consider typical adolescent exploring (the twenty-first-century version of sneaking a look at dad's *Playboy* magazine) to malicious cases with serious consequences made possible by today's technology.

A 2008 study by the National Campaign to Prevent Teen and Unplanned Pregnancy estimated that 22 percent of teenage girls said they had sent or posed for nude or seminude photos. Another poll, at Kidshealth.org, found that 44 percent of high school boys had seen at least one naked picture of a female classmate. Did you get that? It states that 44 percent of high school boys had seen at least one naked picture of a female *classmate.* Not a picture of some supermodel posing for the centerfold of *Playboy* magazine, but a classmate, a girl they see every day. A girl they could potentially date. I wonder how many of those "girl classmates" know that statistic?

A 2009 poll found that one in five teens—guys and girls—sent sexually suggestive pictures via text, and many have received such images, which often originally were sent to someone else. These numbers are even higher when including written sexual content (39 percent of all teens).[7] That's *all* teens.

For example, one case involved a ten-year-old boy who sent a cell phone picture of his genitals to an eleven-year-old classmate "to gross her out." The girl's mother called the police; the boy cried when questioned by police, who concluded he didn't understand the magnitude of his actions and left the matter to his parents.

Another incident involved a sixteen-year-old girl who said she "accidentally" posted a nude photo of herself on a social networking site. A sixteen-year-old boy at her school found the photo and distributed it to a hundred people when she refused his demand to send him more nude pictures. He was charged with a felony and was put on probation.

The results suggest that police generally aren't overreacting to teen sexting, according to Janis Wolak, lead author of the second study. "Some cases that aren't clearly criminal are still worrisome and warrant intervention by parents or others," she said. Did you catch the last phrase of that paragraph? *"Some cases that aren't clearly criminal are still worrisome and warrant intervention by parents or others."* Reading this book is exposing a small portion of a large problem. There's enough information about sexting that an entire book could be written about this alone.

---

[7]   "Teens & Sexting: What Parents Need to Know," Kidshealth.org, 2011 kids' health issue.

What are guys saying about sexting? According to a national campaign to prevent teen pregnancy, 71 percent of guys ages 15–22 say that a girl who has "sexted" is not girlfriend material.

Are you willing to be the "Yes, I will stand up for my daughter" if a boy should ask her to send an inappropriate photo of herself on her phone? Are you going to be the "Yes, I will talk to my son or daughter" about the responsibilities of a phone? Are you going to be the "Yes, I will pay the extra fee on my phone contract" to have the monitoring software on your son's or daughter's phone? Are you going to be the "No, you can't have a cell phone until I feel like you are responsible enough to use it wisely"? Are you going to be the "Yes, I'm going to allow you to have a Facebook page, but I will also have access to your account and a voice in the way in which you use your account"? These are all decisions that you will begin to face sooner than you can say "stop the time machine!"

The following texting experience happened in our home as I was writing this book. I have permission from our daughter to share it with you and have protected the boy who sent these texts by not using his name. He will just be referred to as "boy."

Just to set the scene: our oldest daughter, who is a freshman in high school, has a cell phone. The rule at our house is that the phone goes in our bedroom at night, and she knows we will do random text checks to read her texts at any given time. If she deletes any texts or any part of a conversation, she loses her phone for a week. Well, in September we noticed a conversation with a boy was focused a lot on the clothes she wore, her hair, her makeup, and her eyes. Anytime this boy would text her, he would refer to her physical features. Very seldom did we see just normal teenage chat through their texts. Most of their conversations were about what she planned to wear to school tomorrow. He would ask if she could she take a picture of herself and post it on Facebook so he could see her outfit. I think you get the picture.

Once we realized what their conversations were focused on, we told her that he was not to text her nor was she to text him, and that if he wanted to talk to her he could call her. Several weeks went by, and we noticed he never did call. He couldn't text her because we locked the texting on her phone until we felt she could use it without falling into a trap with this boy. Well, once the texting was turned back on, there was about a month of time that went by that we noticed they didn't text each other. I guess because she didn't call him or text him while her texting was locked, he had lost interest. I was relieved.

Not too long after the moment of relief, we had Thanksgiving break and then moved right into Christmas break. The last weekend of Christmas break I noticed Kenzie texting a lot one evening and told her to put her phone in our room while we played a game as a family. Sometime after the game started, I noticed she was texting under the ottoman. I asked her what she was doing and she said, "Texting. I forgot to put my phone in your room." Well, that was not true, but I didn't want to fight that battle right then. I just had her take her phone and put it in my room. She returned and we finished our game. Before my husband and I went to bed, I did a random text check. It appeared to me that a part of an ongoing conversation had been deleted, but this young man had continued the conversation.

This is what I read (B is for boy):

B: [10:49 p.m.] I gotta tell you that something!
[Kenzie doesn't respond—remember, we parents have the phone]
B: [10:57] Want to know that something you have to do?
B: [11:05] I guess not :b

By this time my husband and I were looking at each other in disbelief knowing in the back of our mind where this conversation was going. My heart was pounding, and I'm pretty sure my neck and face were turning red from fear, confusion, and even anger. I texted back as if I were my daughter.

G: [11:05] What?

B: [11:06] Hmmmm . . . You have to take a picture of you without any clothes on and show me on Tuesday.

Can you just imagine my husband and me sitting up in bed together watching this play out on our daughter's phone? It's a scene I can promise you we don't rehearse in our spare time.

B: [11:10] Ha-ha I'm kidding! (:
B: [11:15] I was just joking!!! I don't even want to see you without any clothes on.
B: [11:17] You think of something. I'll just go to bed. Good night.

Notice we never responded. But he kept on. The next morning:

B: [11:26 a.m.] Good morning ((:
[Remember there has been no response from Kenzie]

Yes, I was absolutely appalled at this point. Thankfully this was the Monday after New Year's Day, and my husband and I both had time to put our heads together and most importantly pray together before our girls woke up.

B: [4:25] KENZIE . . .
B: [4:29] Don't be mad. I was kidding! But its whatever
B: [4:50] I guess we won't kiss.

Remember what I told you about their conversations and what they mostly consisted of? What she wore and how she looked. This boy spent several weeks telling our daughter how beautiful she was and how he loved to see her in this shirt or that shirt, and how he liked it when she wore her hair a certain way. All of this is known as *grooming* as defined by Urban Dictionary: "An act of kindness with an aim to get something in return. For example a telephone number, or perhaps for a favour, or to gain extra contact means with someone, possibly for romantic reasons."

If there's one word you should teach your daughter, teach her that word because it is the way of the world. Younger and younger boys are learning how to use this tactic to reel girls in. Sadly enough, some girls are mastering the art of grooming boys as well. Who wouldn't want to hear all these great things about themselves? Even our daughter with a stable home life, with parents that love her and spend time with her and support her in all she does, wants to hear these things about herself. That's how girls are wired. They thrive from being complimented. But somewhere along the way this conversation went south. It took a turn that our daughter had no idea would lead to what you just read.

After praying together, my husband and I discussed what we should do. Obviously something had to be done. He immediately said he was going to have a talk with the boy and the boy's father. He just didn't know how that was going to pan out. He said he would talk to our daughter and would handle it. I can tell you that in that moment I had a feeling of peace and confidence that he was going to handle it. And the Lord was going to show him exactly how.

I had already planned to take Kenzie shopping that day. But I knew the unavoidable question was coming: "Can I have my phone back?"

What we didn't want was for Kenzie to bolt with anger or mixed emotions that would lead her to cling to the boy more. So David took the phone and put it in a secret location, and as the day went on and Kenzie and I were preparing to leave for an errand, she asked for her phone. My husband sat Kenzie down and began the conversation by telling her he couldn't give her phone to her because we had found some texts from "the boy" that concerned us. He let her look at the texts that had been sent.

Her eyes got big, and she looked very confused and shocked. My husband talked to her about how this boy didn't care about her. He had been telling her all these great things about her because he knows that's what girls want to hear. He told her that if a boy asks you to do something like that, he doesn't really have your best interests in mind. He allowed her to respond, and then decided to continue the conversation later.

One thing my husband did decide when we were discussing how to handle this was that he thought he should talk to her and that I shouldn't be there. Well, of course I kind of felt like I should be there—I mean, we are both her parents, right? But then he explained that he had read in a book written by Dr. Kevin Lehman that in some situations it's best for one parent to handle the situation with the teen so they don't feel like they're being ganged up on—two parents against one teen. Two to one can make me feel intimidated and put me on the defense as an adult. I can see how that would make a hormonal fifteen-year-old feel like she was being overpowered. So, that was a huge step of faith for me to relinquish the right to be there when they talked.

This was definitely a situation that her dad needed to take the lead in. Kenzie left with me, and we spent some time running errands, then she spent the afternoon with friends. Luckily she has great friends who listened to her and echoed the advice her dad gave her, namely that the boy was a jerk, he didn't care about her, and she needed to not talk to him anymore. But at some point she needed to let him know that what he was asking her to do was not something she would ever consider doing. Nor did she feel they could continue texting or talking.

If you are a woman or raising a daughter, you have to know this was hard for her because girls in general want to please people. Even when we know that we can't, we somehow still want to keep the peace. She struggled with the idea she was not being "nice" to someone. She wants to be everyone's friend. We had to explain to her that this was a time she was not in any way obligated to be nice beyond the polite—and I meant very polite—hello in the hallways at school. Some people lose the right to be called your friend. In this case, he certainly lost his right.

A week later my husband texted the boy asking for his dad's cell phone number. In the course of that week, Kenzie made several attempts to talk to the boy about this and tell him she didn't like what he'd asked her to do. Surprise, surprise—the boy didn't want to talk to the girl face-to-face. Texting was much easier for him. It was comfortable for him because it was elusive and detached.

That's one of the reasons texting has taken the course it has. It's an easy way for boys to pursue girls in a way they would never think of doing in person. The boy in this circumstance even said in a follow-up text, "I don't even want to see you without any clothes on anyway." It's too easy to say something in a text that carries more weight than we realize. And it's an easy way for girls to gain attention—the wrong kind of attention. It's all a little too easy, in my opinion. For that very reason parents need to become diligent about talking to their teens about what is going on in their world, do random checks, or purchase accountability software for their teens' phones. Accountability is crucial for teens when it comes to "safe texting." Some adults struggle with using texting in the manner in which it was created to be used. Goodness knows, if adults struggle with the ease and endless possibilities that texting allows, kids will too.

I cannot close out this example without giving credit where credit is due. The Lord has had his hand on Kenzie since before she was born. We have been praying for her and over her every opportunity that we get. My husband and I have diligently sought the Lord for wisdom, guidance, and direction in leading our girls down a path that would one day honor the Lord. As our girls began to enter the adolescent years, it became more difficult for me to have confidence that what I'd been teaching them from the Word was actually sinking in. Teenagers have a way of being elusive, you know. You never know what they are thinking. But I can tell you that in this situation the Holy Spirit had every detail in his hand. From the timing of the text, the time the boy spent grooming our daughter, to the fact that we took her phone up at night and did random text checks. I hadn't done a random text check in a while because I hadn't seen reason to. For some reason I was prompted to do one that night, and I'm thankful I did.

In all of this I keep telling myself that although I wished our daughter had never had one single conversation with this boy that led to the text he sent her, I later found myself thanking the Lord for his sovereignty and his hand through it. This could have erupted into a situation that caused a teenage girl to turn from her parents in rebellion because she didn't want to hear what they had to say about a boy that was telling her she is pretty, he liked her hair, he liked it when she wore this or that shirt, and for crying out loud he was even telling her that he loved her. Really now, you love a girl you won't call on the phone? It turned into a teaching point from the Lord.

I can't help but remind you what the Word says true love is. "Love does not delight in evil but rejoices with truth" (1 Corinthians 13:6 NIV). In another version it is put like this: "Love does not rejoice about injustice but rejoices whenever the truth wins out" (NLT). When someone is pursuing true love, they are denying the lies of the world. The pursuit of true love embraces the truth of pure agape love. Embracing love is denying the flesh and embracing the promise of delight that comes with giving true love. I do not see the denying of the flesh anywhere in the dialogue of the text that I shared with you. Delighting in true love holds a girl's or guy's desire to preserve the most intimate form of love to be shared with one person as a seal of their covenant for one another, higher than falling into fulfilling the fleshy desire of a moment of pleasure. Sexting is just one way so many teens are denying the truth that so clearly defines true love.

Because of this situation, we were able to implement all the communication tips I mentioned earlier in this chapter. Our prayer is that neither one of our daughters will let a lie cause her to forget what God has shown her true love is to be.

If you are feeling a little overwhelmed from reading all of this, please be encouraged by these promises from the Lord: "Yet I am confident I will see the Lord's goodness while I am here in the land of the living. Wait patiently for the Lord. Be brave and courageous. Yes, wait patiently

for the Lord" (Psalm 27:13-14 NLT). "The Lord gives his people strength. The Lord blesses them with peace" (Psalm 29:11 NLT).

Mom and Dad, sexting is not the end all—be all to my world. It is a reality of the land we live in, but I am confident I will see the goodness of the Lord despite the trends of the world. He was faithful to my husband and me when we sought him for wisdom in handling our situation, and he gave our daughter eyes to see the big picture. He gave me—a type A, control-driven-mom—peace throughout the entire situation. Seek him for wisdom and peace in your parenting journey; he is faithful to show himself to you.

Chapter Nine

Safe Sex

"We are living in a sex saturated culture be the ones who teach this to your children— not the culture."

—Ted Cunningham

"Safe sex" is defined by Merriam-Webster's Dictionary as sexual activity and especially intercourse in which various measures (such as the use of latex condoms or the practice of monogamy) are taken to avoid disease (such as AIDS) transmitted by sexual contact—called also *safer sex.*

Some parents believe kids are going to have sex anyway, so why not teach them to have safe sex? You would be surprised at the number of Christian parents who believe the last statement you just read. They represent one segment of the population I am writing this book for.

The following are a few myths and statements I spend time discussing with students when I teach abstinence in the classroom to help them understand the difference between safe sex and abstinence.

- *The world equates sex with love.* That's just one of many myths teens and parents are buying into. Everyone's doing it. The truth is, a lot of people are talking about the sex they are having, but in reality, less than half (48 percent) of all high school students have had sex.

- *"The pullout method will keep me from getting pregnant."* The pullout method typically results in 27 out of 100 people getting pregnant in a year and offers no protection from STDs. The pullout method cannot protect your heart.

- *Some people think it's okay to touch body parts above the waist because by doing this they are not having sex.* Touching body parts above the waist on a girl will charge her hormones to a point where she is then finding herself crossing other boundaries physically because she is unable to keep from going any further.

- *"If I spend the night with him and have sex with him he will love me more."* There are two terms that college students use to describe the girl/guy who is involved in this kind of behavior: "Walk of Shame" and "Walk of Fame." The girl, unfortunately, is the one who wakes up Saturday or Sunday morning, and her car is seen outside the guy's house or she is seen walking across campus with wrinkled clothes, mangled hair, and smudged makeup. And not feeling as good as she did the night before, I can assure you of that. She's walking back to her dorm alone. "Walk of Fame" is used to describe the guy the next day. He wakes up—the girl is gone so he doesn't have to worry about her—he gets his shower, and he walks across campus to the cafeteria for breakfast holding his head high because he got what he wanted last night.

- *"If you love me you will have sex with me."* To which we teach our students to respond with, "If you love me, you will respect my decision to say no." Another good answer to this myth is to say, "You are filling yourself with a false sense of empowerment when you live the lie by giving yourself to another person sexually."

In the New Testament, excluding multiple notations within the same verse, there are thirty-two references to fornication, as indicated by *Strongs' Exhaustive Concordance of the Bible*. A few examples suffice to indicate the tenor of the teachings as a whole.

1 Corinthians 6:18 says "Flee from sexual immorality. All other sins a person commits are outside the body, but whoever sins sexually, sins against their own body" (NIV). When reading this verse I do not see permission for safe sex outside of marriage. It just states, "Flee sexual immorality." Any form of sexual behavior outside of a marriage relationship is considered sexual immorality. Biblical "safe sex" means sexual purity until marriage, followed by monogamy thereafter.

Birth Control Pill

A myth many teens believe is that the pill is completely effective the first day you take it. Different types of birth control become effective at different levels of usage. It can take up to one full month for the pill to become completely effective. It can be ineffective if you miss the pill even one day. Parents, how many teens do you know are responsible enough to take the pill every day at the same time of the day? I have a problem taking my vitamins every day at the same time of the day. How can we possibly put faith in a pill that may or may not be taken the way it was intended to be taken in order to be 100 percent effective in preventing pregnancy? Notice I didn't say "in preventing STDs," because the pill does not protect anyone against any STDs. Notice I didn't say "prevention from feelings of loss, rejection, and depression." The pill is only effective in preventing pregnancy when used effectively.

Condoms

While I'm talking about debunking myths, I should mention condoms. According to a service of the U.S. National Library of Medicine, NIH National Institute of Health, a condom used regularly and correctly should prevent pregnancy 97 percent of the time, and prevent the spread of most STDs. The actual effectiveness among users, however, is only 80-90 percent. This is due to:

- breaks in condom due to manufacturing problems.
- failure to use a condom during each act of intercourse.
- occasional tearing of condom during intercourse.
- semen spilling from a condom during withdrawal.
- waiting too long to put a condom on the penis (penis comes into contact with vagina before condom is on).

Teens carry condoms in their wallet, glove box of their car, and even in the door panel of their car. The following tip was given as a warning: Do not carry condoms in your wallet for long periods of time. Replace them every once in a while. Friction from opening and closing your wallet, and from walking (if you carry your wallet in your pocket), can lead to tiny holes in the condom.

Safe sex or protected sex is used to refer to sex with the use of condoms, pills, or other birth control methods. Are they safe enough for your son or daughter?

Chapter Ten

Boundaries

From our experience with both of our girls, I can say there are times that setting boundaries can sometimes be hard at the time, but seeing the change from the discipline in their future behavior is the reward for this mom. I asked my daughter a week after the texting situation happened to remind me where she had met this boy. She said, "Well, we met at school, but I never talked to him at school. We always talked on Facebook or through texting."

The texting was fairly well monitored by my husband and me. We had already redefined her "communication time" with this young man by telling her she couldn't text him, but if they wanted to talk he was welcome to call her. In three months of "getting to know" each other, he never called her. As this situation came to an end and my husband talked to the boy and his father, we were able to talk to our daughter and explain some things to her that we felt were huge teaching tools that we could not have orchestrated any other way. Now, two months since this learning experience, she has a completely different approach to relationships. An approach with healthier communication boundaries and higher expectations for any future dating opportunities. The Lord clearly allowed this situation to arise in her life because she, like many other teenage girls, didn't believe us when we tried to tell her early on that if that boy doesn't call you and he's just texting you, he really isn't worth your time. He doesn't really like you; he just likes the idea of you.

That's a hard thing to tell your beautiful fifteen-year-old daughter who wants nothing more than to fit in and be well liked by her peers, especially boys! Nonetheless, this situation came to us, and the Lord was very gracious to give us the steps to take in guiding her through it.

Setting Boundaries

"Boundaries—you can't live without them; it's just a plain and simple fact. We have to have them to function in a healthy manner day to day in order to accomplish the bigger things in life." (Dr. James Dobson)

"Hear this, you elders; listen, all who live in the land. Has anything like this ever happened in your days or in the days of your forefathers? Tell it to your children, and let your children tell it to their children, and their children to the next generation" (Joel 1:2-3 NIV). This is an urgent message from God to parents to share their past with their children, telling repeatedly the lessons they learned. Teaching our children the stories of our past can benefit them by teaching them how to avoid the failures we made and encouraging them to repeat the things we did that were successful. A word of caution, though—when sharing experiences you may have had as a child/teen/young adult that you are not proud of or do not want your son or daughter repeating, share them when you think your child is ready to hear them. Seek the Lord on this. Dr. Dobson, licensed psychologist and marriage, family, child counselor, and host of the daily radio program *Family Talk with Dr. James Dobson* recommends waiting until your son or daughter is emotionally mature enough to share details of your past.

It is imperative that you begin talking about "physical" boundaries with your son or daughter early to protect them from sexual abuse. Just like we teach our toddler not to run in the street or touch a hot stove. These are all things we teach our children in their growing years to protect them from harm. Talking about physical boundaries in regard to sex is much the same. It is just as crucial that you maintain an open conversation with them as they develop and their body begins to produce those hormones that naturally cause them to be attracted to and by the opposite sex. When talking to your son or daughter about physical boundaries they want to set in their dating relationship, teach them to set their boundaries, say what their boundaries are (communicate to the person they are dating, or their peers, for accountability), and show their boundaries by not crossing them.

Relating to Them

Moms and Dads, let me paint two pictures of boundaries that I think you will relate to. These are examples that you can use to relate to your son or daughter because they can relate to the feelings communicated in these examples at some level.

Moms, you are going to relate to this example because a house is a woman's domain. Women are very selective regarding who comes into different parts of her home. I know I am. I have been gifted with the love of hospitality. I love to cook for guests and provide a place for others to come sit and enjoy a plate of food and relax with a cup of coffee and chocolate chip pound cake. But, I am not the girl who likes for those dinner guests to come over for dinner, visit, and then ask for a tour of my house.

Please hear me when I say this—if you are reading this and you have been that person to come over and ask, "Can I see the upstairs of your house?" or have said, "I love your kitchen!" then opened up my cabinets to see what was inside, I forgive you. I would never hold a grudge over something like that. This is just an example I think a lot of women can relate to.

If you really want to know what makes me feel uncomfortable, come to my house and ask to see the upstairs. Upstairs! All that is up there are three bedrooms, two bathrooms, and a laundry room. Do you really need to see those rooms to feel welcome in my home? I don't always make it a priority to clean those areas of the house as well as I do the downstairs because I am focusing on the part of my house that will create a warm welcome and inviting environment for guests to want to linger with conversation. Asking to go upstairs and see what is up there makes me feel very uncomfortable. Those places of our house are not for just anybody to see unless they have been invited up.

We have lived in this house for ten years. I struggled with communicating this boundary with grace for more of those years than I care to admit. *But* I have finally been able to effectively communicate that if you come into my home, please enjoy the downstairs and the company that comes with that space. If I invite you up to see the rest of the house, feel honored because it means it's clean and you are getting to see a space in our home that not many are privileged to see. If I don't invite you up, it doesn't mean that I like you any less. It just means that I'm not ready for that part of the house to be seen by anyone that day. I would hope that it's not necessary for you to see all of my house in order to feel as if you were welcome company.

Admitting my own selfish nature, I have been the girl that has been at someone else's house and have asked to see the whole house. I began to realize as I was processing my own dislike of others asking that of me that I might be putting unnecessary pressure on a friend.

To you dads who coach a sport for their son or daughter, or to dads who may be a coach by profession, you know that fields and courts are places that have certain times when they can be occupied by guests. Before a football game, when the stands are just beginning to fill with fans, the football field is occupied by the players of both teams running drills and practicing their passes with the receivers, among the coaches, trainers, and maybe even a camera guy from the local TV station. But you don't see spectators just meandering on the field. Most people know that the field at that time is not open for spectators. Every now and then you might see a young boy excited about the pregame warm-ups run out onto the field. In this case a coach or player may redirect the boy to leave the field.

Before a basketball game the scene is very similar. You see players practicing free-throw shots, drills, layups, and maybe even running a few laps around the court to warm up. The time to walk across a basketball court in an effort to get to the other side is not during pregame warm-up or during a game itself. You walk around. There are even boundary lines that tell you where to walk. The same boundary lines that tell the referees and players when a ball is out of bounds. I think you get the picture here.

Being invited into someone's home does not give us the right to be able to view all of their home. Putting expectations like that on a person may cause them to pull away from the relationship because they may feel you are more interested in seeing what their home looks like rather than focusing on the reason you were invited. Which is most often to get to know you better.

Walking across a football field or basketball court at certain times may put you in danger because there are balls flying in different directions and the players are focused on preparing for a game. I guarantee you they are not focused on protecting spectators from injury.

You may be asking yourself, how does all this relate to boundaries in dating? Setting and communicating boundaries is important for keeping us safe. Communicating boundaries is important because they define the value we put on ourselves and other people. Inviting someone into my home to share a meal with them and visit with them is a way that I communicate to that person that I like them. I want to invest time in getting to know them better. Just because I have invited them over doesn't mean I am obligated to show them all of my house, especially if that makes me feel uncomfortable. In return, the person being invited over should respect the fact that I may not be comfortable showing them all of the living spaces in my home.

Dating relationships are much the same. A girl may want to get to know a guy better so she enjoys talking to him at school. She may even enjoy hanging out with him when there are other people around. Labeling herself as his girlfriend may cause her to feel pressured to do things that couples do in a relationship. Being alone with the guy may cause her to feel uncomfortable, even if he hasn't pressured her to do something she feels uncomfortable doing. Knowing what physical boundaries are acceptable in a relationship makes the relationship more enjoyable for both parties. It takes pressure off of both the girl and boy.

Setting and communicating boundaries is important for keeping us safe from potential STDs, unplanned pregnancy, and emotional distress. Spectators know that when a basketball game is being played they need to walk around the court to get from point A to point B. It is not safe to walk across the court because you put yourself at risk for being hit by a ball or being knocked over by a player. In dating relationships, our son and daughters need to be confident in communicating their physical boundaries in order to protect themselves.

Boundaries in a dating relationship are important because they keep us from giving someone too soon a part of who we are emotionally, and they protect us from physical, emotional, and spiritual consequences.

Will They Understand?

How do we communicate physical boundaries for our sons and daughters in their dating relationships? Being effective in communicating these boundaries begins by relating to our sons and daughters where they are and helping them understand the reason for the boundaries we are encouraging them to set for themselves.

In Acts chapter 8, Phillip, a prophet, is on his way from Jerusalem to Gaza. This passage reads:

> And on his way he met an Ethiopian eunuch, an important official in charge of all the treasury of Candace, queen of the Ethiopians. This man had gone to Jerusalem to worship, and on his

way home was sitting in his chariot reading the
book of Isaiah the prophet. The Spirit told Philip,
"Go to that chariot and stay near it." Then Philip
ran up to the chariot and heard the man reading
Isaiah the prophet. "Do you understand what
you are reading?" Philip asked. "How can I," he
said, "unless someone explains it to me?" So he
invited Philip to come up and sit with him (Acts
8:27-31 NIV)

Later we learn that Philip began with the Scripture the eunuch
was reading and shared the good news of Jesus with the eunuch.
Then we learn that as the eunuch and Philip traveled along the
road, they came across some water, and the eunuch was baptized
by Philip. The story concludes by saying that Philip disappeared
and the eunuch went on his way rejoicing.

I spent time focusing on this story because, parents, we need
to understand that just like the eunuch who was reading about
the prophet Jesus and did not understand what he was reading,
our sons and daughters are hearing mixed messages about what a
Christ-honoring dating relationship looks like. The boundaries
that are being seen by couples on TV, in magazines, and on
the movie screen are not the boundaries that lead to a Christ-
honoring dating relationship. They are hearing some truth about
boundaries in relationships like don't kiss, don't lie down with
a guy or girl, or don't let yourself be alone with someone of the
opposite sex. Don't. Don't. Don't. A very important link to all
of those "don'ts" is the understanding *why* we don't do those
things.

You as their parents can teach them about healthy boundaries
in a relationship. Just as Philip took time to stop during a journey
that he was taking to get from Jerusalem to Gaza, you can take
time to sit down and talk to your son or daughter about physical
boundaries in relationships that will honor the Lord.

At the end of the story we learn that Philip disappears. Mom
and Dad, one day you will not be around to control the choices

your sons and daughters make. But today, while they still live under your roof, you can share truth that teaches them how to make the right choice.

The eunuch was searching for understanding. Philip took the time to explain truth to him. The eunuch received the truth and went on his way rejoicing. That is our goal in teaching our son/daughter why boundaries are important in their dating relationships.

Candle Illustration

One way I teach students about the dangers of sex outside of marriage is with a candle. You can use this illustration with your son or daughter when talking about the dangers of sex or if you are just trying to give them a clear picture of the reason for boundaries. You will need a small votive candle in a glass container, and matches or a lighter.

Lighting a candle that is contained inside a glass container is a great thing. The candle puts off a scent, and the glow from the flame of a lit candle is relaxing. However, lighting a match and just setting it down and letting it burn at will is a very dangerous thing. It can cause a very dangerous effect—an uncontained fire. Sex outside of a committed marriage relationship is dangerous. It can cause STDs, emotional baggage, unplanned pregnancies, and increased risk for depression. Sex within boundaries for the purpose which it is intended is a safe and enjoyable experience.

Another activity you can do with your sons and daughters to help them understand why boundaries are important and where they should be placing their boundaries is with this Stop sign activity. When I go into classrooms to talk to students about boundaries, I use a Stop sign and several poster boards with the stages of progression in a relationship. The first one covers talking (although it may need to include texting for this generation), then the subsequent posters cover holding hands, hugs/kissing, passionate kissing, making out with clothes on, making out with clothes off, oral sex, and sex. I give different students a different poster board to hold up and have them face away from the class so no one can see the one they have. Then I have them turn around and ask another student to come and put the stages in order. Next, I have another student hold the Stop sign and ask them to place it in front of the stage that they would go to if their mom was to be on a date with them. Then I have them move the Stop sign to the stage they would go to if their mom or dad wasn't there. Then I have them place it where they think their boyfriend or girlfriend might want them to place it. When ending this demonstration, I ask them to place the stop sign where they would want their future husband or wife to put their stop sign.

You can do this with your son or daughter—just modify it by writing the stages of a relationship on note cards. Write the word *STOP* onto a separate piece of red construction paper, and set aside some time on a Saturday or maybe one evening during the week when there are no evening activities. Start off by telling them how important they are to you and how they are in charge of their body and the choices they make with their body. You might share your story of boundaries you and your husband set when you were dating. If you didn't have boundaries, do not let Satan fill you with lies that you have no business teaching your son or daughter about boundaries if you didn't have any when you were dating. Remember the promises of the Lord.

Satan wants nothing more than to keep you from teaching your son or daughter the truth about how they are capable of making different choices than you did. When I feel there's something Satan is telling me I can't do, I just repeat over and over in my mind (and even say out loud a time or two until I'm sure he got the message), "Get behind me, Satan!" That usually does the trick for me!

Then move forward. Have your son or daughter tell you where they would place their Stop sign. If it's not somewhere you feel comfortable with, then move into a conversation with them about how you understand they think that's a good place to set their boundary, but you would like for them to place it _____.

Then put the sign where you would like them to place it. For example, if they put their Stop sign on passionate kissing (and a lot of teens will because they feel this is a safe place to be), talk to them about how passionate kissing is just one step away from making out with your clothes on. Making out with your clothes on is one step away from making out with your clothes off. You get the picture.

Then talk to them about how the body works when we are physically attracted to someone, and how our bodies, when interacting in those kinds of ways, are charged with hormones going at light speed, and they are very difficult to stop from going any further. Tell them that once you've moved past a certain boundary physically, it is harder to go back than to go forward.

In his book, *Boundaries with Teens: When to Say Yes, How to Say No*, Dr. John Townsend says, "The boundaries placed on us are for our protection and to allow us to enjoy the freedoms we have . . . . In the past, when most teens did not have much money, culture reflected the values, tastes, and interests of grown-ups. The message to teens was—more or less—'grow up and the world will be yours.' The message seems to be changing to 'The world is yours today, and grown-ups are on the outside.'" Sexual relationships are just one thing that the world is offering our children today. Are you a parent who is willing to let the world shut you out from the influences it is placing on your son or daughter? Or are you going to become a part of the solution by placing boundaries on them for their protection? Are you willing to help them set boundaries for themselves that will allow them to enjoy the freedom of sexual intimacy within the context of a healthy marriage?

Another way to connect with your son or daughter in an effort to help them establish physical boundaries in their relationships is to have a conversation about the lyrics from a popular country song: "Just a Kiss" by Lady Antebellum. I promise it will be worth your time. This is a love song, and the lyrics are a great place to springboard a conversation with your son or daughter about their physical boundaries in dating. You can then compare their boundaries in dating with the boundaries you think are appropriate and acceptable. Sit down and talk about what message this song is sending about the love defined in the song. I have included the chorus for you to understand why I think this song is a great way to connect with your son or daughter about physical boundaries.

I don't want to push too far
Just a shot in the dark that you just might
Be the one I've been waiting for my whole life
So baby, I'm all right, with just a kiss good night

Are you willing to be the "No, you cannot spend the night at their house because I don't know them very well" or because it's best to not spend the night at a house of someone who has a teenage brother? On the flip side, are you willing to be the "No, we cannot have girlfriends spend the night because we have a teenage son in the house"? Are you willing to be the "No, you cannot car date until your dad and I feel like you are mature enough to handle the temptations that car dating brings"? Are you willing to be the "Yes, we would love for your girlfriend to come over Friday night to play games with the family"? Are you willing to be the parent that says "Sure, you can go to the movies with your boyfriend as long as you have several other friends that go with you"? Hopefully, after reading this section you will feel more confident in making these hard decisions. My prayer for every parent is that they are surrounding themselves with a community of parents who reflect their boundaries for their own children. This support system makes raising children at all stages easier.

Chapter Eleven

Dating

D r. Dobson says, "Do not marry impulsively! Remember that the dating relationship is designed to conceal information, not reveal it. So take at least a year to get beyond the facade and into the inner character of the person." Studies from *Research* by the Kaiser Family Foundation show that 91 percent of teens aged fifteen to seventeen that have not had sex said they were influenced by what their parents had taught them about sex. That's your buying power, parents. Remember what I said earlier: "They are saying it, but we are not hearing them." Well, now you know. With knowledge comes a responsibility to seek more knowledge in an effort to impart wisdom. Wisdom that will equip your son or daughter to treasure their gift of sexual activity until they enter a covenant of marriage, with a freedom unlike any other. Parents, it is our responsibility to be the compass for teens and their commitment to abstinence in their dating relationship.

One of teens' consistent gripes over the years is that parents don't take teen relationships seriously. Over and over again, teens have told us that they want parents to know that just because they are young doesn't mean that they can't fall in love. They want parents to know that the feelings they have are very real to them. Let them know that you hear them and that you are respectful of the feelings they have. At the same time, don't be shy about telling them what you think and *why* you think the way you do. Remember though, it should be a conversation, not a lecture.

Dating and Relationships

Hebrews 13:4 says, "Marriage should be honored by all, and the marriage bed kept pure, for God will judge the adulterer and all the sexually immoral" (NIV).

Honoring the marriage bed begins with our dating relationships. Honoring the marriage bed is lived out by how we dress, our body language, the words we say, and how we love others through Christ. Parents, be the voice in your son's or daughter's life that helps them make modest clothing choices and clean language choices, and set appropriate physical boundaries.

It's so important that you don't take for granted the fact that your daughter is smart, she has a strong personality, and she can handle situations. It is great to have confidence in her and to speak confidence to her by telling her you believe in her to make the best choices for herself.

But you can keep her from falling into a trap. Meet her boyfriends. Don't let her be alone at night with her boyfriends. Err on the side of being overprotective and you'll hit it just right, because even if you feel more unreasonable than her friends' parents, remember—they've got the problem of being too naïve. Compared to them you might appear more strict, but you'll be less likely to have problems with your children in the future. Protect her and defend her, and your daughter will know that you love her.[8]

Meet her boyfriend. Yes, that is still a current thing that is happening even in the twenty-first century. When our oldest was in the eighth grade and a boy texted her to ask her to the Farewell Dance, she responded by telling him that he would have to ask

---

[8]   Meg Meeker, *Strong Fathers, Strong Daughters* pp. 234-235

her dad. So the boy asked for her daddy's phone number. He called my husband, and we set up a time for him and his mom to come to our house and meet with David. This tradition and act of protection on David's part became the buzz of conversation at our junior high.

I have to tell you how all of this played out. The boy and his mom came over. The boy and my husband went into the living room, and my daughter and the boy's mom and I went into our kitchen and visited in the breakfast nook. While we were making small talk, my husband was defining his expectations of how we wanted him to treat our daughter on this date. He was to open doors for her. He was to pick her up and drop her off (of course, at this age the boy's dad would be doing the picking up and dropping off). He was to buy her ticket. There was no need to be touching our daughter unless they were dancing, and even then their bodies didn't need to be touching past their hands. He clearly stated there was no reason for them to be exchanging any kissing. And finally he clarified that this was a date to a dance. Going to this dance did not translate into them being in a relationship. It all went splendidly! And this was the first step in our daughter's dating and relationship-building when her daddy had to display his love and protection for her.

Boys need to know early on that they were created to be the initiator in a relationship. With that comes responsibility: respecting girls, showing manners that reflect God's image of a respectable young man, showing they have been taught how to be chivalrous. Chivalry is slowly fading as girls become more aggressive in relationships. Dads, you need to be the one to model and expect the chivalrous behavior from your son. You, Dad, are the one who models how a woman should be treated by how you treat your wife. Mom, the same goes for you with how you show respect to your husband.

When talking to girls—or texting girls as they do so much now—boys need to be mindful of emotional language. They need to guard their emotions when developing a relationship at any level with a girl. Girls should be given a line of defense.

Dads, role-play conversations with your daughter so she can have comebacks that provide protection and allow her an out. Dating isn't forever; it's practice for marriage. Before teens date, they should be taught that they very well could be dating someone else's future spouse. The Bible gives wise advice when it says: "Above all else, guard your heart, for it is the wellspring of life" (Proverbs 4:23).

Don't Start Too Early

Song of Solomon 2:7 reads, "Do not arouse or awaken love until it so desires." In some translations the word *arouse* is replaced with *stir up*. Simply put, we are repeatedly advised through the Song of Solomon to not arouse or awaken love until it so desires. It's not wise to put young children into situations that will entice their desire for romance or sexual pleasure. Exclusive dating as early as ages eleven through sixteen is too early, in my opinion. You have read the statistics. I shared trends of sexual behavior and how young they are starting.

This is a list of boundaries you can discuss with your sons and daughters. Use some of your own dating experiences to break the ice when talking about them. I have been told by teens that they like to hear their parents tell stories of their high school and college dating life. It's even better when you tell a story that shows your son or daughter that you made a mistake but learned from the mistake and made different choices.

1. Set physical boundaries early in the relationship. Respect each other's boundaries. Girls, if you are dating someone who does not respect your physical boundaries, he's not worth the regret that will come if you cross a boundary. Guys, remember you could be dating someone else's future spouse. Respect her as you would want your future spouse to be treated.

2. Take it slow. Keep it casual. An inheritance gained hastily at the beginning will not be blessed at the end

(Proverbs 20:21). Don't let your relationship move so fast that it burns out early on.

3. Keep your emotions in check when sharing feelings. Don't share insecurities during early stages of dating. Some will exit the relationship out of fear you are going to be a constant downer.

4. Give the other person some room to breathe. Don't text, call, or initiate the next time you see each other so often that the other person tires of you quickly. Give the other person time to spend with their friends and family.

5. If you think you have found the love of your life, be cautious in sharing this feeling. The other person may not have come to this conclusion.

6. Guys, learn the art of chivalry. You know—call the girl, ask her out; don't wait for her to ask you out. Open the door for her. Pull her chair out for her at the table. Pay for her meal. Offer to carry her books or gym bag for her at school.

7. Guys, if you know a girl has a "crush" on you, ask her questions that lead her to tell you more about herself. What is your favorite kind of food? What kind of movies do you like to watch? (Hint: they will most often say "comedy romance." You will learn to tolerate a good "romantic comedy" just to sit next to a girl you like.)

8. Guys and girls, encourage the person you like or are dating in the things they are interested in. If she plays soccer, ask her about her position. Ask her about the last game she played. If he plays football or golf, ask him questions about his last game.

9. Guys, compliment the girl you like for something she said or did. Make it a point to find something besides her physical attributes to compliment her on.

10. Guys, girls like to feel safe. Girls, overdramatic responses are not attractive in the long run. Keep your drama for your girlfriends.

11. Don't allow yourself to be alone in a car with someone of the opposite sex until you are mature enough to make wise decisions with the temptations that can come with being alone in a car with someone you are attracted to.

12. Make it a rule to not be home alone with anyone of the opposite sex.

13. This last one is from Dr. Dobson's book *Love Must Be Tough*: Sexual familiarity can be deadly to a relationship. In addition to the many moral, spiritual, and physical reasons for remaining virgins until marriage, there are numerous psychological and interpersonal advantages as well. Though it's an old-fashioned notion, perhaps, it is still true that men do not respect "easy" women and often become bored with those who have held nothing in reserve. Likewise, women often disrespect men who have only one thing on their minds. Both sexes need to remember how to use a very ancient word. It's pronounced "no!"

I mentioned earlier that our daughter learned from her texting experience. Just this week she took another step of growth in defining who she is and what she expects from her relationships. A boy she liked asked her after several weeks of talking and getting to know her if she wanted to be his girlfriend. We have told our girls that there really is no reason to label themselves as someone's girlfriend because they can't really see that other person outside of school or places we are going to be, so why the label? We have also told them that putting that exclusive dating puts pressure on you.

She didn't really understand what we were telling her. She didn't rebel and do things behind our back, but she did tell him she would be his girlfriend. This is one of those decisions as a parent of a teen we decided to continue gently opposing through conversation with her, but we didn't tell her she had to change her decision. We continued to have conversations with her about our reasons for not putting the girlfriend/boyfriend title on a relationship. One week after they officially became boyfriend/girlfriend her boyfriend changed his status on Facebook to say he was in a relationship with Kenzie. We noticed she wasn't really comfortable with that but she did the same. As soon as she changed her status, I began to get phone calls from others that were concerned for her. Friends were asking: Why is she in a relationship with someone? Don't you know what kind of drama comes with being in a relationship? Doesn't she know that it's so much better to not date exclusively that young? To which I answered, "Yes, she knows all these things; we have talked about this with her. We know she can't go anywhere with him, so we really aren't concerned. She's going to have to come to the conclusion on her own that putting a label on a relationship comes with pressures and that it's not all it's cracked up to be."

I continued to pray she would hear the advice we were giving her and that she would remove the relationship status on her own. I prayed she would have the boldness to talk to her boyfriend and tell him she doesn't feel it's necessary to have the title of boyfriend/girlfriend to get to know each other. The Lord answered every one of my prayers!

Just four days after she posted that they were in a relationship, she came home and we sat on the back porch and talked about her feelings. She shared with me that after changing her status he began to walk her to every class, and some of her peers began to ask her if they had held hands or kissed yet. He never put any pressure on her to do those things, but her peers were putting pressure on her just by asking. After talking about her feelings and gently reminding her of the benefits in doing the right thing even when it was hard, she went inside and changed her relationship status on Facebook.

This is when, as a mom, I can't say enough how proud I am of her. I wanted so badly to go change that status myself when she posted it, but I also know that everything I have read about teenagers is that as parents we have to communicate our opposition on certain issues but allow them to make their own choices and be there to help them if they fall as a result of their choice. Obviously, if there was a choice one of our girls was making that would cause them harm or someone else harm, we would intervene, but the choice to be someone's girlfriend wasn't causing her any harm because we knew we had control over how much time they would be spending together.

After removing the relationship status on Facebook, she texted her boyfriend to tell him what she had done and why. She very simply told him she wasn't ready for the commitment of being someone's girlfriend because of the pressure that came with that commitment. Of course he responded by saying, "I respected you by not putting any pressure on you to hold hands or do anything else." She explained to him that the pressures were coming from other peers, and she wanted to get to know him without the pressure. He was thankful she still wanted to be friends, and she is relieved to not have any more pressure from her peers. It's a win–win situation!

The way this played out was exactly how we have told her things go with high school dating relationships. By taking a stand for her boundaries and kindly stepping away from a girlfriend/ boyfriend relationship, she defined to her peers that she is not that kind of girl who is willing to do physical things with a boy just because she is the boy's girlfriend. She had a peer at school question why she would become someone's boyfriend and two weeks later break up with him for no apparent reason. To which she answered, "I just don't want the pressures that come with a committed relationship." The boy that was questioning her responded by saying, "So now I know what kind of girl you're not." Confused, Kenzie asked, "And what kind of girl am I not?" He responded with, "I know you are not a slut."

Parents, do you see now how even making a choice like breaking up with someone because you don't want the pressure of having to hold hands or kiss because you are boyfriend/girlfriend can set a precedent for teens and the standards they have for their dating relationships? This is the kind of example I will share in the classroom to encourage students that they can make the hard decisions and there is good that comes with setting a high standard for themselves. We have told both our girls that it's so much better to not put a title on a relationship, because oftentimes in the breakup process you risk losing a friend. Thankfully it did not end up that way.

Another bit of encouragement before you read on. Look at what James has to tell us about knowing the commandments of the Lord and living them out: "The one who peers into the perfect law of liberty and fixes his attention there, and does not become a forgetful listener but one who lives it out-he will be blessed in what he does" (James 1:25 NET). The Lord gave us the commandments in Deutoronomy 5 as boundaries for living a life that brings him glory. Not one of the commandments given is meant to be impossible to live out. Although we may all find ourselves tempted to dishonor one of the commandments, we have the power of Christ to give us the strength to not fall to that temptation—*if* we choose to allow ourselves to live through his power.

How to Deal with Pressure

"Be watchful, stand firm in the faith, act like men, be strong" (1 Corinthians 16:13 ESV).

I love that the ESV version says "act like men." Dads, did you get that? Pray for your sons to be watchful and strong. Be an example for them. Teens say that they feel pressure in their relationships to have sex. In fact, many think that having sex is the price of entry for a relationship, or the thing that will keep a relationship together. As adults, we know that these are both untrue and, even worse, it's extremely unhealthy thinking. Your advice should be direct: If sex is the price of a relationship, find someone else.

A very common question from teens is, "How can I tell I'm in love?" Many parents make the mistake of hearing this question from their child and immediately respond with "You're too young to be in love!" (Cue "loud humming/fingers in the ears" posture from Mom and Dad). The truth is, though, who's to say? The feelings your teen has are as real to them as yours are to you and aren't any less important. The key here is to help them understand what they're feeling and make good, responsible decisions. You have a wonderful opportunity to share your knowledge and guide your child—don't put them on the defensive by dismissing their feelings.

Instead, consider starting the conversation by asking your teen the questions like: Is the attraction just physical or something more than that? Does he/she accept you as you are? Is he/she supportive of your interests and the things that are important to you? Do you feel that the relationship is balanced or that one person is doing all the giving and the other person is doing all the taking? Is the emphasis on *us* more than *me*? Are you confident that you can stand up for your own values and beliefs, even if your partner disagrees?

Chapter Twelve

DADS

"We need to teach our daughters to distinguish between a man who flatters her, and a man who compliments her.

A man who spends money on her, and a man who invests in her.

A man who views her as property, and a man who views her properly.

A man who lusts after her, and a man who loves her.

A man who believes he is God's gift to women, and a man who remembers a woman was God's gift to man.

. . . And then teach our boys to be that kind of a man."

—Abby Johnson: Pro-Life Advocate

Dads, you have an incredible amount of influence over your son and daughter. Although they may not act like it, they are looking to you for protection. Developing a healthy relationship with your daughter while she is young is crucial to being able to speak truth into her life when she will need it most—in her teenage years. Boys will be prowling, and your daughter will need someone to be her protector. Your son will need a role model to show him how to treat the girls he is dating.

The protection shown by my husband through the texting situation has provided our oldest daughter with a higher sense of worth and value in her daddy's eyes. And don't be mistaken—teenagers talk. The boys at her school know that her daddy went and talked to the boy that texted her asking her to send a picture of herself without any clothes on. It wasn't easy, I'll tell you. My husband didn't want to have to go to that boy's house and tattle on him to his dad, but it was worth it because now Kenzie knows her daddy cares enough about her to do that, and the boys at her school know where her boundaries are and that she has her dad backing her up.

Dads, you are an invaluable influence on your son and daughter. Dr. Michael Gurian, author of *The Wonder of Boys*, says that "every time you raise a loving, wise, and responsible man, you have created a better world for women. Women (today) are having to bond to half-men, with boys who were not fully raised to manhood, don't know how to bond, don't know what their responsibilities are to humanity, and don't have a strong sense of service." A great place to start sharing the value of a father's wisdom is in Proverbs chapter 4. It's entitled "A Father's Wise Instruction" in the Life Application Bible NIV. The following passages are just a few that are mentioned in the Word (from the English Standard Version) that will present many opportunities for you to have discussion with your son or daughter about honoring their sexual purity:

- **Romans 13:13: "Let us walk properly as in the daytime, not in orgies and drunkenness, not in sexual immorality and sensuality, not in quarreling and jealousy."**
- **1 Corinthians 6:18: "Flee from sexual immorality. Every other sin a person commits is outside the body, but the sexually immoral person sins against his own body."**

- 1 Corinthians 10:8: "We must not indulge in sexual immorality as some of them did, and twenty-three thousand fell in a single day."
- Galatians 5:19: "Now the works of the flesh are evident: sexual immorality, impurity, sensuality."
- Ephesians 5:3: "But sexual immorality and all impurity or covetousness must not even be named among you, as is proper among saints."
- Colossians 3:5: "Put to death therefore what is earthly in you: sexual immorality, impurity, passion, evil desire, and covetousness, which is idolatry."
- 1 Thessalonians 4:3: "For this is the will of God, your sanctification: that you abstain from sexual immorality."
- Jude 1:7: "Just as Sodom and Gomorrah and the surrounding cities, which likewise indulged in sexual immorality and pursued unnatural desire, serve as an example by undergoing a punishment of eternal fire."

Dads and Daughters

I am going to give you a few pieces of advice that were included in Dr. Dobson's book *Bringing Up Girls*. They were originally written by Harry Harrison and published in a book entitled *Father to Daughter: Life Lessons on Raising a Girl*. I have just included a few:

- Take part in her life now. Don't wait until she's fifteen to try to develop a relationship.
- Never forget that supportive fathers produce daughters with high self-esteem.
- Make her a Valentine's Day card—every year. (I remember getting Valentine's Day cards from my dad even after I was married.)

- Keep her secrets—this way she will begin to trust men.
- Praise her often. Let her know you love her the way she is. If you tell her this often enough, she might remember it throughout adolescence.
- Remember, society is teaching her its values 24/7. You need to be more determined to teach her yours.
- Teach her patience, kindness, and tolerance. If you don't, many years from now you'll wish you had.
- Think before you speak. Even when you don't mean to, you can end up hurting her feelings.
- Remember, teenage girls spend hours in their room doing something. No man has ever really figured out what that something is.
- Once she begins to develop physically and sexually, don't pull away from her.
- Get to know her friends. Middle school marks the zenith of peer influence.

Dads and Sons

I didn't want to ignore the father/son relationship. Hear are some tips for dads to help build their relationship with their sons.

- Be available. Time = love in any relationship. Especially in a father/son relationship.
- Begin teaching chivalry at a young age. You can start as early as four teaching your son to open the door for his mother, or asking guests if they would like something while you are up getting something for yourself. Modeling any behavior desired is most effective when teaching it.
- Praise him when you see him accomplish something. Build his ego with a healthy dose of humility. Again, modeling the character you are trying to produce will

make it easier for him to understand the reason for that character trait and more likely to be achieved.

- Work on a project with your son. This creates an opportunity for one on one time to connect and accomplish something together.
- Attend sporting events together. This is a time for you to share a common interest with your son.
- Carve time to fish or hunt together. Sitting and waiting for the catch of the day or the hunt of the season is a perfect time to talk about things that are not easily talked about when others are around. The time you are sacrificing to be with your son will not go unappreciated.
- Talk to him about the changes you notice going on with his body. Ask him if he has any questions. Relate to him by sharing experiences you remember during the awkward years of puberty. Even if he continues to say no, let some time pass and ask again. A time will come that he may surprise you with a question that could initiate a life changing conversation.
- Talk to him about the importance of setting his own boundaries in his relationships and respecting physical boundaries in his dating relationships. Explain why it is important to ask girls that he dates what their boundaries are and those boundaries.
- Model how he should be the initiator in relationships by how you initiate with your wife.
- Teach him to value the heart of a woman by showing this kind of love for your wife through kind words/ actions.
- Teach him how to manage money. Once he is old enough to begin working a part time job, have a conversation with him about the importance of tithing, budgeting and wise spending habits.
- Challenge him in his relationship with the lord.

- Challenge him to pray even if it makes him uncomfortable. He will be the leader of a family one day and prayer is the foundation of the family.

Chapter Thirteen

What in the World do I say?

Sexual thoughts or feelings become sinful when you act on them inappropriately. Ask yourself if you've made the transition as a parent from knowing the truth and knowledge to sharing the truth and knowledge, from theory to application. It takes courage and faith and a complete dependence on Christ to be the messenger of this kind of truth to your son or daughter. Expose them to that which you want them to experience—a Christ-centered lifelong reward of pure intimacy with their spouse. Ask yourself this question: "Is Jesus worth more than a moment of pleasure-comfort-disobedience-adultery?" Ask your son or daughter this question.

Colossians 3:5 says "Put to death, therefore, whatever belongs to your earthly nature: sexual immorality, impurity, lust, evil desires and greed, which is idolatry." Well, there must be something important here because the first sin Paul tells us to put to death is sexual immorality. Sex outside of marriage is sexual immorality.

So which is it going to be for you? Are you going to be in the business of letting the sin of sexual immorality kill you, or your son or daughter, either spiritually or physically with disease or chances of not being able to have a family later in life?

O my people, hear my teaching; listen to the words of my mouth. I will open my mouth in parables, I will utter hidden things, things from of old—what we have heard and known, what our fathers have told us. We will not hide them from their children; we will tell the next generation the praiseworthy deeds of the Lord, his power, and the wonders he has done. He decreed statues for Jacob and established the law in Israel, which he commanded our forefathers to teach their children, so the next generation would know them, even the children yet to be born, and they in turn would tell their children. Then they would put their trust in God and would not forget his deeds but would keep his commands. They would not be like their forefathers—a stubborn and rebellious generation, whose hearts were not loyal to God, whose spirits were not faithful to him. (Psalm 78:1-5)

We want to believe that we are always doing a great job to keep our son or daughter safe and training them to make the right choices. We talk to them about the risks in drinking and smoking, and how to get out of a burning house. But there is one thing that many parents today are not talking to their children about and that is sex. Sex is something that everyone will experience at some point in their life. Why wouldn't parents want to be the ones to talk to their children about sex? We are the experts, after all. We did have sex at least once to bring that child into this world. Talking to our kids about sex is not just talking to them about the *act* of sex; it's breaking down the stages our body goes through to prepare to have sex, and it's talking about the purpose of sex and the dangers of sex.

The beginning of this book focused on facts, some activities, and conversation starters you can have with your teenagers. Now we are going to take a look at how you start to build the foundation of a healthy sexual education for your son or daughter that is rooted at home with Mom and Dad. The stronger a foundation you lay at home, the better equipped your son or daughter will be to fight the media and their peers in this uphill battle.

Be on your knees. Lay a foundation. Begin with the truth. Set healthy boundaries. Allow freedom. Be available. Be knowledgeable. Be approachable. Be flexible. Did I mention be available? Time is going to be a huge investment you will make in your son or daughter all through their developing years, especially their teen years.

Remember what I said in the opening chapter about not really liking the adolescent stage of parenting? No matter what stage of parenting we are in, the objectives have changed, but the purpose is still very much the same: Fill their heart with truth, love, and understanding of who they were created to be.

Paul admonishes us in 1 Thessalonians 4:1-8:

> Finally, brothers, we instructed you how to live in order to please God, as in fact you are living. Now we ask you and urge you in the Lord Jesus to do this more and more. For you know what instructions we gave you by the authority of the Lord Jesus. It is God's will that you should be sanctified; that you should avoid sexual immorality; that each of you should learn to control his own body in a way that is holy and honorable, not in passionate lust like the heathen, who do not know God; and that in this matter no one should wrong his brother or take advantage of him. The Lord will punish men for all such sins, as we have already told you and warned you. For God did not call us to be impure, but to live a holy life. Therefore, he who rejects this instruction does not reject man but God, who gives you his Holy Spirit.

We don't know the level of consequences God is going to give us. But we do know what his Word says about the blessings of not engaging in sexual sin before marriage.

You may be saying, "What if I didn't wait?" Before you begin to talk to your son or daughter at any age about sexual development, it is a very good idea to make sure to clean out our own baggage if there is any, if you made mistakes you are ashamed of and don't want your son or daughter to make. Spend some time in prayer seeking the Lord for forgiveness (if you haven't already). Ask the Lord for wisdom to prepare you to know when and how to share with your child about your past. Dobson suggests always being honest, but at the right time. Not every child will be ready to hear the same information at the same age. You can use your past mistake as an example of what should not be done, then point out what you did to change and why that change was more beneficial and honored the Lord. What a great picture of repentance.

You might also ask, "What if they ask questions I'm not ready to answer?" Tell them you will get back with them. That's okay.

The Scriptures say it; the statistics I shared with you speak to it; media is screaming it in pictures, words, and music. Our sons and daughters live in a volatile generation. Seductive imagery is in their face coming from many angles. Their innocence begins to be compromised at a young age. The culture isn't doing anything to cut it at the quick. In fact, culture is pulling them into its influence of believing that living a promiscuous life is going to offer more to them than living a life of purity. The pressure to become sexually active is all around teens; everyone around them assumes they are going to be sexually active, or mocks them if they choose to remain a virgin. This type of pressure provides a breeding ground for failure.

Connection

Nearly 40% of girls ages 15–17 have had two to five sexual partners, according to a study done by the Kaiser Family foundation. How do we fight against the strong pull of the media and influences from peers to tone down the sexual normalization through Internet, texting, and social media? Teens are looking for alternative ways to connect. Bootie call, friends with benefits, and hooking up, are all terms used for casual sex. Otherwise known as connecting. They are using their sexuality as that alternative method. I mean, sex is a means of connecting, right?

How We Connect

"Sex within the context for which it was intended—lifelong, monogamous marriage—is always safe. This is the message our kids need to hear from the earliest days of childhood! Anything less is worse than third-rate!"[9]

The limbic system of our brain stores our emotional and sexual memory, not our heart. Smells, music, and sexual intimacy are all things that turn the limbic system on. When engaged in sexual intimacy, our body releases a chemical known as dopamine. Dopamine creates a sense of peace and pleasure, all at the same time. Dopamine is a neurotransmitter that activates pleasure centers in certain parts of the brain. Simply said, "The dopamine-affecting caffeine in chocolate is part of why you feel happy when you eat it."[10] When your body experiences pleasure, the limbic system—a part of the brain—is washed with dopamine, which makes you want more of whatever you just had. Much like an addiction. Dopamine is a pleasure attachment. It attaches you emotionally to whatever brought you that pleasure. Whether the pleasure came from a friend or stranger, an addiction is created by the release of dopamine.

Another chemical released during sexual intimacy is oxytocin. Oxytocin can be released as the result of simple skin-to-skin touching, such as holding hands or kissing, and it is released

---

[9] Dr. James Dobson, from his book *Solid Answers.*
[10] "How Caffeine Works," an article by Marshall Brain, Charles W. Bryant, and Matt Cunningham.

during sexual orgasm. Oxytocin is the bonding chemical our brain is washed with during sexual intimacy. So, all in that one act of "connecting" through sexual intimacy, our brain is being washed with an addictive chemical followed by a bonding chemical—no matter the source of sexual intimacy, whether it be friend, acquaintance, or spouse. Oxytocin is the same chemical released during childbirth and when a mother nurses her baby. Its purpose and intent is to act as a bonding agent between mother and baby.

What do you think? The apostle Paul wrote, "Do you not know that he who unites himself with a prostitute is one with her in body? For it is said, 'The two will become one flesh'" (1 Corinthians 6:16). Lauren Winner, author of *Real Sex*, says Paul is really saying, "Don't you know that when you sleep with someone your body makes a promise whether you do or not?"

Sadly enough, many teens are drawing a boundary line in their emotional connections through sexual promiscuity that can never be erased. Once a bond has been made with a sexual partner, it is never broken. That is why the Lord created us to be addicted to our spouse. Take a look at what these Scriptures from the New Living Translation say about a husband and wife becoming one. I think they clearly express God's divine design for sexual intimacy and the emphasis that needs to be placed on preserving our sexual purity until we are in a covenant married relationship.

- **Genesis 2:24: "This explains why a man leaves his father and mother and is joined to his wife, and the two are united into one."**
- **Mark 10:6-9: "But 'God made them male and female' from the beginning of creation. 'This explains why a man leaves his father and mother and is joined to his wife, and the two are united into one.' Since they are no longer two but one, let no one split apart what God has joined together."**

- **Ephesians 5:31-32: "As the Scriptures say, 'A man leaves his father and mother and is joined to his wife, and the two are united into one.' This is a great mystery, but it is an illustration of the way Christ and the church are one."**

What the media is not telling its audience is that the true reality that comes with that type of connection is not the reality they are longing for. It's not the reality they have imagined in their mind. When teens figure out that this lifestyle of communication and form of connecting don't offer the results they are after, they will start asking, "Now what?"

This is where having a strong relationship and an ongoing conversation with your kids is helpful. Many parents struggle to get to this place with their kids. Teens are young men and young women, not just young kids anymore, and we can't control what they're thinking, yet we need to give them input along the way.

Action Steps

Ages three through five: Between the ages of three through five it is important that our children see their bodies as a gift from God. They recognize their differences from the other gender and that God made us different, but we were all made in his image, and we are loved by him just the same. This is the stage in development in which it is important that children begin to see that the framework for family as designed by the Lord. Children between the ages of three and five start to understand this framework through beginning to learn and understand some of the basics of human reproduction, where a baby comes from, and how they come out of mommy's tummy. Your voice inflection, body language, and response to their inquiries about their body parts will play a large part in how they retain the information you are teaching them about their body.

For me, I see bath time, potty training, and playtime as excellent teaching moments for vocabulary development—a vocabulary lesson of utmost importance. You, Mom and Dad, are teaching your son or daughter the names of the parts of their body that they will one day use to glorify the Lord in an act of intimate connection with their future spouse. We teach them the function of those body parts, how and why we keep them clean. In these teachable moments while they are young, we are building trust and a comfort zone in which they can come back to us with more questions about their body as it goes through changes. In addition to all of that, you teach your toddlers the importance of not letting others touch their private parts. We conquer the task of training them to use the restroom in the right place and at the right time.

Whew! As if that isn't enough, some may ask the monumental question: "Where did I come from?" You might answer, "God made you!" Then hopefully leaving it at that for then. But oftentimes that will not be enough information for the ever-inquisitive four-year-old mind. When you ask back a question like, "What do you mean?" it allows your son or daughter to tell you what they already know about the question they've just asked. Oftentimes they may have already had this conversation with a peer and they're just wanting to talk about it with you. An answer you can give that often fills the child's curiosity and answers the question at their cognitive level is this: "You grew in mommy's tummy. Mommy has a special place where babies grow. It's called the uterus. When it was time for you to come out, you came out of my body."

Your child may ask, "How did God put me in your tummy?" A friend of mine answered this question by telling her child that when a mommy and daddy go to bed at night, sometimes they hug and kiss real tight and their bodies come close together and daddy plants a seed inside of Mommy and then God makes it grow. To which a child might ask, "Where does daddy get the seed?" A very awkward question, but a good one at that. I would say it like it is. "Daddy's penis makes the seed go into Mommy." Oftentimes that will be enough. Depending on the age of a child, they may not ask any more questions—which means they've heard enough to satisfy their curiosity. Lucky you. Now you get to wait for the next time you are running errands or folding laundry and your sweet little one comes up with another brilliant question.

I don't know about you, but I have to wipe my brow again. Being a parent is something else, huh? All this talk about where babies come from and using these words with our toddlers is mind-boggling. Hear me when I say this: you are the mom and dad. You choose when you think your son or daughter is ready to hear any of the answers to the questions they are asking. Each child is different. Each child is going to ask a different number of questions. Some may ask early on; others may never ask, and you may have to give the information whether they ask or not. We have one of each. One of ours is not at all interested in asking questions but more than happy to have a conversation about most any topic if we initiate it. The other will ask all kinds of questions and even evaluate whether or not we have given accurate information.

Ages five through eight: Build on what you taught your three—to five-year-old. You will want to begin introducing the upcoming changes their body will be going through as it prepares to become a woman or man. Mom, as your daughter begins to approach the age of eight, is a good time to talk about the impending occurrence of their cycle. Talk to your daughter about these changes. Tell her they are natural changes. Let her know that these changes are just the beginning stages of how the Lord has planned for her body to change from a young girl into a young lady. Ask her if she has any questions. Say something like, "That's a great question; I'm glad you asked that. I know this is a hard subject to talk about." You might even go ahead and get a small bag ready with panty liners and put it under her bathroom sink. Share your story of the first time you had your cycle to help alleviate fear and worry that she is abnormal during this awkward time of development.

This is the age that your son or daughter will enter school, develop social circles, and begin to be exposed to what others have to say about sexuality. Yes, even in kindergarten some children will share too much information at school—oftentimes incorrect information. Positive first messages are always more powerful. Spend time talking to your son or daughter about sex early on before they are bombarded with the world's view on sex. It will give you a stronger foundation for the relationship you are developing to maintain open conversation about the changes that will continue to face your children leading up to, through, and beyond puberty into dating and relationships.

A note to parents with girls: While writing this book, a conversation came up with my oldest that I think cannot go unnoticed. We had the talk about her period the summer between her third and fourth grade. I chose to talk about it then because so many girls are beginning to start their cycle earlier and earlier. I wanted her to be knowledgeable if her peers were talking about it and prepared should it happen to start for her. One thing I didn't really spend enough time on was explaining that she would bleed all day for several days. I just said she would need to be prepared for her body to bleed for several days. She didn't understand it meant she would be bleeding all the time during those several days. I just wanted to add that because it was something she brought to my attention that confused her. Details are important.

Dads, when your daughter begins to enter the third grade, you should initiate the habit of knocking on her door so you don't accidentally walk in on her and see her without her clothes on. Talk to her about making it a habit to begin closing her door when she is undressed or changing clothes. There's nothing more embarrassing for an eight—to eleven-year-old developing her breasts than for dad to see her without her shirt on. This is a great time for Mom to take her daughter to get a sports bra to wear, or a training bra. Make it a special time. Get a soda or hot chocolate and talk about how special these changes are. Again, just like sharing your first menstrual cycle story with her, share your first impression of a bra and help clear the air while purchasing her first bra. This, too, will be a building block in the foundation that will help keep an open door for this conversation as she continues to develop.

Ages eight through eleven: This has been by far my second favorite time in parenting because changes are taking place in our daughters' bodies that have led them back to needing me for something. They have needed me to take them shopping for their first bra. They have needed me to talk to them about why their friends are so moody one day and then not moody the next. I love that they have needed me for these conversations.

Moving on, at this age we want to continue to build on the basics of sexual intercourse and God's purpose in creating us with different purposes as a man and woman. At this age it is good to build on the purpose God intended for sex to be reserved for marriage. Dads, your daughter by the age of six will love the idea of a date night with you. Some towns have annual daddy-daughter dances. If you ever have an opportunity to take your daughter, I promise it will be an investment worth your time. Taking her to events like this provides you with the opportunity to treat her like a lady and demonstrate the appropriate chivalry that should be expected by those who may choose to date her in the future. Capitalize on setting aside time to take her on dates beginning at age five or six and don't ever stop.

This is also a good age to begin introducing them to the activities that I mentioned earlier. Begin to point out messages that the media is sending about sex, and develop conversations that will give you opportunity to feed them truth about the importance of fighting off what the world is telling us about sex and what the Bible has to say about sex and relationships.

Modeling your belief about sex and relationships is crucial as well. Children know when you are just feeding them a line of bull and when you are buying into something. Living proof through watching Mom and Dad toe the line makes it easier for our sons and daughters to make the hard choices when they are up against the forces of the messages from media. Just sheltering our children from the realities of how the world and media are portraying sex may leave them defenseless against the attacks they will receive from the world.

Ages eleven through fourteen: Once again, continue to build on the concepts you have been introducing. This is the age when some girls have had a cycle, and some are having a regular monthly cycle. Some girls are already sexually active. Boys are going through the whole morphing phase: hair growth, penis is changing, voice is changing, legs are growing, feet are growing. Your pantry is never full enough to keep up with your son's bursts of hunger. He is showing off in front of girls—that's the testosterone kicking in. And he's pretty clumsy. Man, poor boys. Dad, be available and ready to talk to him about all these changes and to guide him in proper care of his continually changing body. Remind him how to treat his mother. Model that treatment. It may seem redundant, but it will pay off in the end.

This is the age that your son and daughter are hearing more than you would have ever thought from school about some of their peers that are "boyfriend and girlfriend" or "going together." This is also the age that most kids get their first cell phone. This is the age that your son or daughter is taught to become responsible for the feelings they will have for the opposite sex. It is normal. They are going to see someone of the opposite sex and like the way they look. Your job in the beginning of this stage is to deposit truth regarding the need to maintain self-control, respect for others and themselves, and boundaries.

God's Word deals with real people and their real problems. The passage in 1 Corinthians 7:8-9 acknowledges the reality of human sexual drive. Verse 37 speaks of human will and indicates that mastery of one's sexuality is obtainable. Verses 1-2 are typical of verses setting forth the practical tone of God's design for the proper use of human sexuality. This is a good time to talk about the boundaries I mentioned with the activity earlier on in the book. It is also a good time to talk about peer pressure. Begin to help them develop relationships with other kids you see making good choices. Be available to have talks, and encourage them when they make good choices. This is when you learn to respond and not react. Listen even when what you are hearing hurts your heart. Then respond lovingly with truth and redirection. Don't talk about them with other parents. Trust is *huge* at this age, and it will be so crucial to the rest of the time they are at home with you.

For girls and boys, their thirteenth or fourteenth birthday is a great time to present them with a purity ring. Having talks with them about God's purpose for sex leading up to this monumental birthday is a very good way to celebrate this time of independence. Our oldest that has one says it's a good reminder for her to see hers on her finger, that she has made a promise to her daddy and me and to the Lord to wait. It's also a visual reminder to the prowling boys or girls, that they made a commitment to wait. It represents a symbol of protection.

Moms, you may have had several of those bra-shopping trips. Dads, I hope your calendar is sprinkled with time to be with each of your children. Yes, boys like to "date" their dad too. Except they may prefer a burger and shake over the Panini and salad from Panera Bread your daughter prefers. Regardless of their likes, make time to spend time with them one on one. Mom and Dad, make certain that even if you can't sit around your own dining room table at least five nights a week to share a meal together you are sitting at a restaurant table to fill in the gaps.

Dobson says that families that share meals together have less chance for relationship breakdown. Something about eating a meal together brings another level to that relationship you are establishing that will leave an open door for conversation. Our favorite meal of the week is Saturday morning. My husband makes breakfast—eggs, bacon, fruit, potatoes, toast, juice, and coffee. It's great food, and we usually spend time talking about the week or what is coming up, or oftentimes it ends with my husband between the girls and the three of them searching YouTube for the latest *Marcel the Shell* episode. Memories. Trust. Communication. A bond being strengthened.

As Mark Gregston said in his article "Teaching Purity in a Seductive Culture," this is the perfect time to sit down with your teen and openly talk about what's acceptable and what's not. So, if you have been building your relationship with your teen along the way, your child may be more receptive to what you are hoping to accomplish. Even with good relationship-building, kids don't always listen to or follow our standard. Parents, if you see your teen acting slightly outside of the standard, it's okay to choose your battle and say, "I don't like it, but I'll let it go." But it's important to clarify the standards for modesty and your expectations.

Expectations aren't a list of rules. They're taught in conversations, and modeled by the example of your lifestyle. Instead of showing our kids how to live in a zoo, we have to be teaching them to survive in a jungle. Sometimes a child tells a parent, "I don't believe in the things you do, I don't behave the way you do, it's my body, I'll do what I want." This becomes a different conversation. Instead of talking about expectations of the household, you might have a practical conversation about the Scriptures and show how a lack of modesty can hurt relationships.

Deviating from God's plan always ends with pain and failure. We need our kids to know that God doesn't merely say, "Don't!" God says, "Don't get hurt!" The Scriptures are a great place to start because they show our teens their value. Ask the questions: "What would your future husband want in you?" "What would your future wife want in you?" As your teens begin to define this for themselves, stay engaged with them. Model the life you want for them, and help them sort through their confusion. In the context of relationship, teens will see this instruction not as judgment but as love and connection; just what they're looking for.

Recently, I was given an article from *The Dallas Morning News* entitled "Beyond the Birds and the Bees: Grade Schools Urged to Teach about Body Parts and Sexual Orientation." The basic premise of this article was to educate the reader that schools across America are inconsistent in how they address this topic. It is being proposed in some states that a curriculum be developed and implemented that addresses teaching sexual orientation as "the romantic attraction of an individual to someone of the same gender or a different gender." This is just one of the sexual guidelines being addressed by a coalition of health and education groups. The purpose of implementing such curriculums is to help schools build sequential foundation that will better help teens as they grow into adults. It's also used as an initiative to help prevent bullying in schools. In response to the initiative, Valerie Huber, executive director of the National Education Abstinence Association, said that, like the antismoking campaign of the last few decades that has had success, sex education should focus on abstinence. "This should be a program about health rather than agendas that have nothing to do with optimal sexual health decision-making," she said. "Controversial topics are best reserved for conversations between parent and child."[11]

Ages fifteen through eighteen: You are now charting a different course. I'm still charting that course. So far I have learned that Dr. Dobson, Jack Graham, Kevin Lehman, and Chip Ingram all have sound advice on raising teens. The following is just some information on dating and relationships that I think will be most helpful in this stage.

What a Guy Really Wants in a Girl

A friend of mine, in an e-mail survey she conducted, gathered these responses from a pool of Christian college-aged young men:

1. The biggest thing that I try to get girls to understand is that even the slightest bit of "extra" skin can really put a guy over the edge in his thought life. Low-cut shirts (not even showing cleavage), short skirts, or especially bikins during the summer all make a guy's mind start to spiral.
2. A good verse to ponder when considering your clothing choices and the effect they may have on others

---

[11]   *Dallas Morning News* 1/18/2012 Sex Education World section

is Hebrews 3:13: "But encourage one another daily, as long as it is called today, so that none of you may be hardened by sin's deceitfulness." Is anything about your outfit encouraging others to sin?

3. I always appreciate when a girl dresses modestly, and there's a certain amount of respect that goes hand-in-hand with that appreciation. That's just one less stumbling block I have to deal with, and for that I'm thankful.

4. Don't wear clothes that show anything that it would be inappropriate for a guy to touch in public. If a guy can see it, he has probably already touched it a few times in his mind . . . just a thought.

5. "Modest is Hottest" really is true. I look at girls who dress like Megan Fox and wouldn't want anything to do with them. It's like they are giving themselves away to everyone and anyone who wants a piece. As a future husband (Lord willing), I don't want my future wife to have been lusted after by other men. Physical beauty becomes cheap when it is whored out to everyone. Guys can tell who is really pretty without the girl having to show a lot of skin.

6. No pictures of yourself in a bikini on Facebook! One of the young men said he has lost respect for a number of girls who have posted pictures of themselves in a bikini.

What a Girl wants in a Guy

1. A heart for the Lord
2. Ask her what her boundaries are & respect them
3. Open the door for her
4. Call her
5. Pick up the tab
6. Surprise her with a hand written letter
7. Initiate conversations about her interests

8. Sense of humor
9. Protect her
10. Apologize when you are in the wrong
11. Look her in the eyes when you are talking to her, more importantly look her parents in the eyes when speaking to them
12. Extend a handshake to her parents every time you take her out
13. Let her see how you love your mother

These are just a few things that girls look for in a guy. I would imagine if you feel like you need more guidance in how to treat a girl in your dating relationships you can ask a girl and she or her parents will be happy to tell you.

Moms and Dads, I am including a Modesty Checklist that you should go over with your daughter and help her to begin modeling the standards defined by these guidelines. Join her in this adventure and model the guidelines in support of her efforts to dress modestly. Encourage her to wear a cami or tank top under low-cut shirts to help her still be able to be creative in her style, with modesty. Here is the checklist:

1. **Underpants check: If you can sit or bend over and your panties show, put on a shirt that is long enough to cover them up or choose a different style of jeans.**
2. **Belly button check: Can you see your belly when you lift your arms above your head?**
3. **Ask yourself—or better yet, ask Mom / or Dad—how short is too short?**
4. **Ask: Is my shirt cut too low?**
5. **Ask: Are my clothes too tight?**

Have your son or daughter write down attributes they want their future husband or wife to have. They may write something like this:

- I want my future spouse to be a Christian and love the Lord. I want him to be a _____.
- I want my future husband to have that messy-hair look and a scruffy beard.
- I want my future spouse to look good. I mean, I don't want to marry someone I don't think is good-looking.
- I want my future spouse to have a sense of humor.
- I want my future husband to treat his mother and my mother with kindness and respect.
- I want my future husband to be a good listener.

You want your kids to have an idea of what they like, otherwise they are at risk for just settling for anything.

Proverbs 11:22 (NIV) says, "Like a gold ring in a pig's snout is a beautiful woman who shows no discretion." The overarching theme from the responses seen is use discretion when choosing what to wear. Exposed skin does cause a guy to have lustful thoughts and it really is not attractive to be with a girl who is showing too much skin.

Parents, be in the know when it comes to what guys and girls are looking for in each other. Have a dialogue with your adolescent about them. Oftentimes hearing from Mom or Dad what a boy might be thinking can help girls rethink how they act in front of boys. The same is true for guys.

Conclusion

To circle back to where we started—teens really do want to hear from their parents about relationships, even if they don't always act like it. And it's never too late (or too early) to start these conversations—there are appropriate messages and conversation-starters for every age group. Make sure that your sons and daughters know that you are always there for them, that you always have a sympathetic ear, and that no topic is off limits. Never underestimate the great need that children feel—at all ages—for close relationships with their parents and for their parents' guidance, approval, and support.

This may mean some extremely awkward or difficult conversations. It may mean resisting, with all of your willpower, the urge to cover your ears and pretend your child did not just ask you that question. But know that it's just as awkward and difficult for them to broach the subject as it is for you to hear it. Address their concerns and questions with respect and sensitivity and, over time, both you and your teen will become comfortable having these conversations.

Parents, when we put our focus on the Lord and his promises and his wisdom, he will give us the victory. Even when we can't see reason in the battle, the Lord knows the outcome. Trust him. Joshua trusted him and had his people walk around the walls of Jericho with their mouths shut. Faith can be as equally contagious as fear if you let it be. He is waiting on you to hold up your end of the bargain and believe in him. Even when it comes to your sons and daughters. Everything we face can be dissolved by the Word of God when we stand on his promises. Psalm 16:8 says,

"I have set my eyes on the Lord always." When we are slipping in our journey as parents, his promises are a certain cure of the blues of defeat.

These are some passages that I have been clinging to in this journey of parenting. I have included them as a tool for you to hang on to his promises and remember to keep your eyes on the prize:

- James 1:5 (NIV): "If any of you lacks wisdom, he should ask God, who gives generously to all without finding fault, and it will be given to him." (When reading James 1:5, fill in these blanks for yourself and for your son or daughter):
  I need wisdom for _____

  _____

  (Insert your son/daughter's name) needs wisdom for _____

  _____

- Colossians 2:4-5 (NIV): "I tell you this so that no one may deceive you by the fine sounding arguments. For though I am absent from you in body, I am present with you in Spirit! And delight to see how orderly you are and how firm your faith in Christ is."

- Psalm 57:2 (NLT): "I cry out to God Most High, to God who will fulfill his purpose for me."

- Philippians 4:6 (NLT): "Don't worry about anything; instead, pray about everything. Tell God what you need, and thank him for all he has done."

- (Psalm 78:5-8 NLT): "For he issued his laws to Jacob; he gave his instructions to Israel. He commanded our ancestors to teach them to their children, so the next generation might know them—even the children not yet born—and they in turn will teach their own children. So each generation should set its hope anew on God, not forgetting his glorious miracles and obeying his commands. Then they will not be like their ancestors—stubborn, rebellious, and unfaithful, refusing to give their hearts to God."

- **1 Chronicles 16:11-12 (NIV): "Look to the LORD and his strength; seek his face always. Remember the wonders he has done, his miracles, and the judgments he pronounced."**
- **1 Peter 5:7 (NIV): "Cast all your anxiety on Him because He cares for you."**
- **Isaiah 26:3 (NIV): "You will keep in perfect peace those whose minds are steadfast, because they trust in you."**
- **Habakkuk 3:1-2 (NIV): "LORD, I have heard of your fame; I stand in awe of your deeds, O LORD. Renew them in our day, in our time make them known; in wrath remember mercy."**
- **Psalm 27:13-14 (NIV): "I am still confident of this: I will see the goodness of the LORD in the land of the living. Wait for the LORD; be strong and take heart and wait for the LORD."**

When looking at Proverbs 4, we see that there are five times that our children are reminded to listen to the wisdom of their father and take it to heart, to guard their heart. All of chapter 4 is written to children specifically. Chapter 5 is written to address sons avoiding immoral women. Dads, take it on as your responsibility to study that chapter with your sons to equip them with future wisdom for marriage.

Something I do for our girls to keep Scripture in front of their eyes is I put note cards on their nightstand or their magnet board once a week, the same verse I am praying for them that week. It has worked very well because they have both told me they look forward to getting the verses, and neither of them has thrown them away. This week's verse is Proverbs 3:21-22: "My son, preserve sound judgment and discernment, do not let them out of your sight. They will be life for you, an ornament to grace your neck."

There is so much more that could be said about saying no to the sexual pressures of the world before marriage. I trust that you will glean from other authors and fellow parents who have paved the road before you. I have included a list of resources I recommend while you are on this journey that I hope are helpful. My deepest desire for you after reading this book is to be filled with knowledge that you can pass on to other parents and, most importantly, your children.

Afterword

What if you have read all of this and you are the parent of a teenager who has already had sex or is in a relationship that you see could be leading to sex? Remember what I mentioned in the section on pornography? Don't react, but respond. Respond with love. Respond with grace. Respond with prayer. Respond with a plan to help your son or daughter navigate their way out of that kind of a relationship and back into a lifestyle of abstinence. Be prepared to provide an accountability partner for your son or daughter.

When talking to students, I explain that it is very easy to make a choice in our relationships that we regret. Oftentimes the regret they feel in making the wrong choice leads them to think it's too late to change their behavior and make the right choice in their future relationships. It's never too late to make a better choice. It's so much better to recognize the mistakes in past relationships that can be avoided in the future.

Several things I would advise you to do as a parent in this situation. Remember the words of the Lord. Remember his love. Remember his grace. Remember what repentance is. Remember what mercy is. Go to the Word for strength to live out the love, mercy, grace, and forgiveness you will need to love your son or daughter through their time of changing the decisions they have made in past relationships. Guide your son or daughter through the process of acknowledging their sin in their relationships, asking the Lord to forgive them of their sin, repenting from their sin, and walking forward in the knowledge, strength, love, and grace of our Lord. You may even relate to your son or daughter by sharing a story about a time you made a mistake in life that you knew had to be taken to the Lord for forgiveness. This is a great opportunity for your teen to see how the Lord has been a father of grace, mercy, and unfailing love for you in your own life.

Transparency goes a long way with our children. Parents are just as human as children are. We have all made mistakes. Thankfully, we know there is a God of mercy and grace who will love us through those mistakes and is faithful to forgive us of our mistakes when we acknowledge them.

I have included the following Scriptures to help guide you and your son or daughter through the process of renewing their relationship with the Lord.

> **"Never will I leave you; never will I forsake you." So we say with confidence, "The Lord is my helper; I will not be afraid." (Hebrews 13:5–6 NIV)**

Did you get that? "The Lord is my helper; I will not be afraid." When we went through the sexting situation with our daughter, I had to remind myself of this passage because my husband and I needed a helper to handle that situation with wisdom. We had to depend on the Lord to give us the words to speak and the grace to walk through that with our daughter. He was faithful to help us through.

> **May the Lord of peace Himself give you peace at all times and in every way. (2 Thessalonians 3:16 NIV)**

It was the Lord's peace that I had when I knew David needed to have the conversation with McKenzie without me about the text messages from the boy who had texted her. It is the peace of the Lord that gets me through parenting on a daily basis. Let him be your peace.

Cast all your anxiety on Him because He cares for you. (1 Peter 5:7 NIV)

The Lord is never going to tell you he is weary of hearing the burdens of a mother's or father's heart. He is waiting for you to trust him with your burdens so he can show you just how much he cares for you. Trust him.

The Lord is good, a refuge in times of trouble. He cares for those who trust in Him. (Nahum 1:7 NIV)

Again, the Lord is waiting for you to trust him.

Give thanks to the Lord of lords, for his steadfast love endures forever (Psalm 136:3 ESV)

So I will bless you as long as I live; in your name I will lift up my hands. (Psalm 63:4 ESV)

When we focus our attention on praising the Lord even in the midst of trial, we are glorifying him. When we are praising the Lord in the midst of trial, we are tuning out the lies of Satan and eclipsing them with the truth of the Lord. Even in the midst of seeing your son or daughter make a choice you would rather them not make, thank the Lord for your son or daughter. Thank the Lord for his enduring love that lasts forever. In the time of thankfulness, we are renewed with the strength of the Lord to get through a trial.

This passage in James is a great place to start with showing your son or daughter the faithfulness of the Lord to forgive our sins. This is also a great passage to remind your son or daughter of the importance of confessing sin to another person.

And the prayer of faith will save the one who is sick, and the Lord will raise him up. And if he has committed sins, he will be forgiven. Therefore, confess your sins to one another and pray for one another, that you may be healed. The prayer of a righteous person has great power as it is working. (James 5:15-16 ESV)

Guide your son or daughter through a conversation of recognizing the sin in sexual immorality. Read Ephesians 1:7-10 to them. Have them read it back to you. Ask them if they have any questions about the promise that is given to them in this passage.

In him we have redemption through his blood, the forgiveness of our trespasses, according to the riches of his grace, which he lavished upon us, in all wisdom and insight making known to us the mystery of his will, according to his purpose, which he set forth in Christ as a plan for the fullness of time, to unite all things in him, things in heaven and things on earth. (Ephesians 1:7-10 ESV)

There is therefore now no condemnation for those who are in Christ Jesus. For the law of the Spirit of life has set you free in Christ Jesus from the law of sin and death. For God has done what the law, weakened by the flesh could not do. By sending his own Son in the likeness of sinful flesh and for sin, he condemned sin in the flesh, in order that the righteous requirement of the law might be fulfilled in us, who walk not according to the flesh but according to the Spirit. (Romans 8:1-4 ESV)

Romans 8:1-4 is a great reminder to any believer that Christ has fulfilled the penalty for our sin through his death. Further on in Romans chapter 8 in verse 6, it says, "For to set the mind on the flesh is death, but to set the mind on the Spirit is life and peace." After reading this passage to your son or daughter, you have a great opportunity to move into a time of prayer over them to help them have the strength to turn from the sin they are struggling with and turn to the Lord for strength to live in the truth of his Word.

This is also a great time to introduce the idea of having an accountability partner who can help them stay the course—someone who can lead them in truth and keep them focused on the Spirit instead of the temptations that may arise in future relationships. I cannot say enough how important it is to relate to your son or daughter by telling them of a time in your life that you may have had someone hold you accountable to something. Whether it be eating habits, spending habits, choosing your words wisely—whatever it may be—I have seen our kids respond to challenges that we give them with a positive attitude when we follow up with relating to them through sharing a challenge we have faced. Mom and Dad, this is a time when you are going to have to be okay if they don't ask you to be their accountability partner. Teens are growing into their own faith. This time of growing into their own faith incorporates others that they have seen walking in line with God's truth influencing them in areas of their life. You lay the foundation with truth, then let them navigate their own path.

Understanding the grace of the Lord is the healing portion in recognition of sin, repentance of sin, and moving forward with the Lord in an effort to not fall back into that pattern of sin. I love the way 1 Corinthians 1:4-9 is written in The Message Bible:

Every time I think of you—and I think of you often!—I thank God for your lives of free and open access to God, given by Jesus. There's no end to what has happened in you—it's

beyond speech, beyond knowledge. The evidence of Christ has been clearly verified in our lives. Just think—you don't need a thing, you've got it all! All God's gifts are right in front of you as you wait expectantly for our Master Jesus to arrive on the scene for the Finale. And not only that, but God himself is right alongside to keep you steady and on track until things are all wrapped up by Jesus. God, who got you started in this spiritual adventure shares with us the life of his Son and our Master Jesus. He will never give up on you. Never forget that.

What a great way to encourage your son or daughter that the Lord will never give up on them. Remind them that you will never give up on them either.

Resources

Preschool (Ages 3-5)
The Princess and the Kiss
The Squire & the Scroll
— by Jennie Bishop

God's Design for Sex
— by Carolyn Nystiom

This is a four-book series for children and parents to read together beginning at age three going all the way up to age fourteen.

1. *The Story of Me* (Ages 3-5)
2. *Before I was Born* (Ages 5-8)
3. *What's the Big Deal? Why God Cares about Sex* (Ages 8-11)
4. *Facing the Facts: The Truth about Sex & You* (Ages 11-14)

Questions Kids ask about Sex
— by Melissa R. Cox and the Medical Institute for Sexual Health

Running the Rapids: Guiding Teenagers through the Turbulent Waters of Adolescence
— by Dr. Kevin Leman

Strong Fathers, Strong Daughters
Your Kids at Risk
— by Dr. Meg Meeker

So You're About to Be a Teenager
Parenting Today's Adolescent
    —by Barbara & Dennis Rainey

Bringing Up Girls
Bringing Up Boys
Parenting Isn't for Cowards
    —by Dr. James Dobson

Every Young Woman's Battle
Preparing Your Daughter for Every Young Woman's Battle
    —by Shannon Ethridge

Sex180—The Next Revolution
    —by Chip Ingram/TimWalker

And the Bride Wore White: Seven Secrets to Sexual Purity
    —by Dannah Gresh

On Becoming Preteen Wise
    —by Gary Ezzo & Robert Buknam MD

5 Conversations You Must Have with Your Son
5 Conversations You Must Have with Your Daughter
    —by Vicki Courtney

Bibliography

The Associated Press. "Beyond the Birds and the Bees". The Dallas Morning News, 2012, p. 12 A-Sex Education-World Section.

Azam, Sharlene. *Oral Sex is the New Goodnight Kiss: The Sexual Bullying of Girls*. Bollywood Filmed Entertainment, 2009.

Bishop, Jennie. *The Princess and the Kiss*. Warner Press, 2000.

Bishop, Jennie. *The Squire and the Scroll*. Warner Press, 2009.

Bob Hoose, review of "The Lucky One". Plugged In Movie Review. http://www.pluggedin.com/movies/intheaters/lucky-one.aspx. 2012.

Brain, Marshall, Charles W. Bryant, and Matt Cunningham. "How Caffeine Works". http://ieet.org/index.php/ieet/moore/brain20070322.

Centers for Disease Control and Prevention. "STDs". http://www.cdc.gov/std/stats07.

Centers for Disease Control and Prevention. "Sexual Risk Behavior: HIV, STD, & Teen Pregnancy prevention," http://www.cdc.gov/healthyyouth/sexualbehaviors/index.htm, 2011.

Clear Play DVD Player. http://www.clearplay.com/howclearplayworks.aspx.

Condom Facts. National Institutes of Health. http://www.nlm. nih.gov/medlineplus/ency/article/004001.htm.

Courtney, Vicki. *5 Conversations You Must Have With Your Son.* B&H Publishing Group, 2011.

Courtney, Vicki. *5 Conversations You Must Have With Your Daughter.* B&H Publishing Group, 2008.

Cox, Melissa R., and Medical Institute for Sexual Health. *Questions Kids Ask About Sex.* Revell, 2007.

Cunningham, Ted. *"We are living in a sex saturated culture. Be the ones who teach this to your children—not the culture."* Men at the Cross, www.menatthecross.org, 2010.

Divorce Rates/Cohabitation Statistics. http://www. usattorneylegalservices.com/divorce-statistics.html.

Dobson, James C. *Love Must be Tough.* Waco, TX: Word Books, 1983.

Dobson, James C. *Solid Answers.* Carol Stream, IL: Tyndale House Publishers, 1997.

Dobson, James C. *Bringing Up Boys.* Carol Stream, IL: Tyndale House Publishers, 2001.

Dobson, James C. *Parenting Isn't for Cowards.* Carol Stream, IL: Tyndale House Publishers, 2007.

Dobson, James C. *Bringing Up Girls.* Carol Stream, IL: Tyndale House Publishers, 2010.

Dobson, James C., http://www.facebook.com/#!/ myfamilytalk.

Ethridge, Shannon. *Every Young Woman's Battle*. Waterbrook Press, 2004.

Ethridge, Shannon. *Preparing Your Daughter for Every Woman's Battle*. Waterbrook Press, 2005.

Evans, Tony. http://www.oneplace.com/ministries/the-alternative. 2012.

Ezzo, Gary, and Robert Bulkman, MD. *On Becoming Preteen Wise*. Parent Wise Solutions, Inc. 2001.

Garrett, Rose. "Is Your Child Sexting? What Parents Need To Know". http://www.education.com/magazine/article/child-sexting-parents. 2009.

Gentile, Douglass, and Walsh, David. *A Normative Study of Family and Media Habits*. Minneapolis: National Institute on Media and the Family, 2002.

Jack Graham and Deb Graham. *Courageous Parenting*. Crossway Books, 2006.

Graham, Jack. http://www.oneplace.com/ministries/powerpoint/listen.

Gregston, Mark. "Teaching Purity in a Seductive Culture". www.heartlightministries.org. 2012.

Gresh, Dannah. *And the Bride Wore White: Seven Secrets to Sexual Purity*. Moody Publishers, 2004.

Gurian, Michael. *The Wonder of Boys*. Tarcher, 1997.

Harrison, Harry. *Father to Daughter: Life Lessons on Raising a Girl*. New York: Workman Publishing Co., 2003.

Haywood, David; Scott, Hillary; Davidson, Dallas; Kelley, Charles. *Just a Kiss*. Warner/Chappell Music, Inc.,

EMI Music Publishing. http://www.lyrics.com/just-a-kiss-lyrics-lady-antebellum.html.

Hooten, Jeff. "The New Virgins". www.troubledwith.com/Web/groups/public//@fotf_troubledwith/documents/articles. 2004.

Innefective Contraception. http://www.contracept.org/withdrawal.php.

Ingram, Chip, and Walker, Tim. *Sex 180-The Next Revolution*. Baker Books, 2005.

Johnson, Abby: Pro-Life Advocate. www.facebook.com/person, 2011.

Johnson, Patrick. "A Force Behind the Lower Teen Birth Rate: MTV's 16 and Pregnant". USA/Society.

The Christian Science Monitor, 2010.

The Kaiser Family Foundation. "Virginity and The First Time". http://www.kff.org/entpartnerships/3368-index.cfm, 2003.

The Kaiser Family Foundation. "National Survey of Teens on HIV & AIDS". http://www.kff.org/youthhivstds/upload/National-Survey-of-Teens-on-HIV-AIDS.pdf

Kaissan, Mary A., *Girls Gone Wise in a World Gone Wild*. Chicago, IL: Moody Publishers, 2010.

KidsHealth. "Teens & Sexting: What Parents Need to Know". http://kidshealth.org/parent/positive/issues_2011/2011_sexting.html, 2011.

KidsHealth. "Condoms & Birth Control Facts". http://kidshealth.
org/teen/sexual_health/contraception/bc_chart.html.

Legrand, Connie. WSPA-TV, 2009.

Leman, Kevin Dr. *Running the Rapids: Guiding Teenagers Through
the Turbulent Waters of Adolescence.* Tyndale House Publishers, Inc.
2005.

Mayle, Peter. *Where Did I Come From?* New York: Kensington
Publishing Co., 1977-2000.

Meeker, Meg. *Strong Fathers, Strong Daughters.* New York:
Ballantine Books, 2006.

Meeker, Meg. *Your Kids at Risk.* Regency Publishing, 2007.

Murphy, Ann Pleshette. "How to Decode Slang your Teen uses
Online". http://abcnews.go.com/GMA/Parenting/webspeak-
101-parents-decode-teen-internet-slang/story?id=11684997,
2010.

Murray, Andrew. http://wildernessprc.org.

Nystiom, Carolyn. *God's Design for Sex.* Navpress, 1984.

The National Campaign to Prevent Unplanned Pregnancy, and
cosmogirl.com. "Results of Sex & Tech Survey". http://www.
thenationalcampaign.org/sextech.

The National Institute on Media & Family. "Media Influences
on Youth /Teens & Sex". http://www.crisisconnectioninc.org/
teens/media_influence_on_youth.htm.

Oxford Dictionary Online. s.v. "Sexting". http://oxforddictionaries.
com/definition/sexting?region=us&q=sexting

Parker, Trey (Writer), and Parker, Trey (Director). *Fourth Grade*, Episode 0412, South Park, New York: Comedy Central, 2000.

Perry, Katy; Gottwald, Lukasy; Martin, Max; Levin, Benjamin; McKee, Bonnie. "Teenage Dream". Warner/Chappell Music, Inc., Downtown Music Publishing LLC, 2010. http://www.lyrics.com/teenage-dream-lyrics-katy-perry.html.

Rainey, Dennis and Barbara. *So You're About To Be A Teenager.* Thomas Nelson, 2003.

Rainey, Dennis and Barbara. *Parenting Today's Adolescent.* Thomas Nelson, 2003.

Ropelato, Jerry. "Pornography Statistics 2003". http://internet-filter-review.toptenrevsiews.com.

Tiernon, Anne Marie. "Oral Sex Survey". http://www.wthr.com/story/4560345/oral-sex-survey?clienttype=printable, 2012.

Tooley, Heather. "Texting: 30 Teen Slangs Parents Should Know of Text Messaging Abbreviations".

http://telephone-voice.factoidz.com/texting-30-teen-slangs-parents-should-know-of-text-messaging-abbreviations.

Townsend, John Dr. *Boundaries With Teens; When to Say Yes How to Say No.* Zondervan, 2006.

Urban Dictionary Online, s.v. "grooming". http://www.urbandictionary.com/define.php?term=grooming.

Urban Dictionary Online, s.v. "safe sex". http://www.merriam-webster.com/dictionary/safe%20sex.

Urban Dictionary Online, s.v. "walk of shame". http://www. urbandictionary.com/define.php?term=walk%20of%20shame.

Urban Dictionary, s.v. "walk of fame". http://www. urbandictionary.com/define.php?term=walk+of+fame.

Winner, Laura. *Real Sex*. Brazos Press, 2005.